Infrastructure Decisions
Complete Self-Assessment Guide

The guidance in this Self-Assessment is ba: best practices and standards in business pr and quality management. The guidance is judgment of the individual collaborators listed in the Acknowledgments.

Notice of rights

Trademarks

Table of Contents

About The Art of Service

The Art of Service, Business Process Architects since 2000, is dedicated to helping stakeholders achieve excellence.

Defining, designing, creating, and implementing a process to solve a stakeholders challenge or meet an objective is the most valuable role… In EVERY group, company, organization and department.

Unless you're talking a one-time, single-use project, there should be a process. Whether that process is managed and implemented by humans, AI, or a combination of the two, it needs to be designed by someone with a complex enough perspective to ask the right questions.

Someone capable of asking the right questions and step back and say, 'What are we really trying to accomplish here? And is there a different way to look at it?'

With The Art of Service's Standard Requirements Self-Assessments, we empower people who can do just that — whether their title is marketer, entrepreneur, manager, salesperson, consultant, Business Process Manager, executive assistant, IT Manager, CIO etc... —they are the people who rule the future. They are people who watch the process as it happens, and ask the right questions to make the process work better.

Contact us when you need any support with this Self-Assessment and any help with templates, blue-prints and examples of standard documents you might need:

http://theartofservice.com
service@theartofservice.com

Acknowledgments

This checklist was developed under the auspices of The Art of Service, chaired by Gerardus Blokdyk.

Representatives from several client companies participated in the preparation of this Self-Assessment.

In addition, we are thankful for the design and printing services provided.

Included Resources - how to access

Included with your purchase of the book is the Infrastructure Decisions Self-Assessment Spreadsheet Dashboard which contains all questions and Self-Assessment areas and auto-generates insights, graphs, and project RACI planning - all with examples to get you started right away.

How? Simply send an email to
access@theartofservice.com
with this books' title in the subject to get the Infrastructure Decisions Self Assessment Tool right away.

You will receive the following contents with New and Updated specific criteria:

•   The latest quick edition of the book in PDF

•   The latest complete edition of the book in PDF, which criteria correspond to the criteria in...

•   The Self-Assessment Excel Dashboard, and...

•   Example pre-filled Self-Assessment Excel Dashboard to get familiar with results generation

•   In-depth specific Checklists covering the topic

•   Project management checklists and templates to assist with implementation

INCLUDES LIFETIME SELF ASSESSMENT UPDATES

Every self assessment comes with Lifetime Updates and Lifetime Free Updated Books. Lifetime Updates is an industry-first feature which allows you to receive verified self assessment updates, ensuring you always have the most accurate information at your fingertips.

Get it now- you will be glad you did - do it now, before you forget.

Send an email to **access@theartofservice.com** with this books' title in the subject to get the Infrastructure Decisions Self Assessment Tool right away.

Your feedback is invaluable to us

If you recently bought this book, we would love to hear from you! You can do this by writing a review on amazon (or the online store where you purchased this book) about your last purchase! As part of our continual service improvement process, we love to hear real client experiences and feedback.

How does it work?
To post a review on Amazon, just log in to your account and click on the Create Your Own Review button (under Customer Reviews) of the relevant product page. You can find examples of product reviews in Amazon. If you purchased from another online store, simply follow their procedures.

What happens when I submit my review?
Once you have submitted your review, send us an email at review@theartofservice.com with the link to your review so we can properly thank you for your feedback.

Purpose of this Self-Assessment

This Self-Assessment has been developed to improve understanding of the requirements and elements of Infrastructure Decisions, based on best practices and standards in business process architecture, design and quality management.

It is designed to allow for a rapid Self-Assessment to determine how closely existing management practices and procedures correspond to the elements of the Self-Assessment.

The criteria of requirements and elements of Infrastructure Decisions have been rephrased in the format of a Self-Assessment questionnaire, with a seven-criterion scoring system, as explained in this document.

In this format, even with limited background knowledge of

Infrastructure Decisions, a manager can quickly review existing operations to determine how they measure up to the standards. This in turn can serve as the starting point of a 'gap analysis' to identify management tools or system elements that might usefully be implemented in the organization to help improve overall performance.

How to use the Self-Assessment

On the following pages are a series of questions to identify to what extent your Infrastructure Decisions initiative is complete in comparison to the requirements set in standards.

To facilitate answering the questions, there is a space in front of each question to enter a score on a scale of '1' to '5'.

1 Strongly Disagree

2 Disagree

3 Neutral

4 Agree

5 Strongly Agree

Read the question and rate it with the following in front of mind:

**'In my belief,
the answer to this question is clearly defined'.**

There are two ways in which you can choose to interpret this statement;
  1. how aware are you that the answer to the question is clearly defined
  2. for more in-depth analysis you can choose to gather

evidence and confirm the answer to the question. This obviously will take more time, most Self-Assessment users opt for the first way to interpret the question and dig deeper later on based on the outcome of the overall Self-Assessment.

A score of '1' would mean that the answer is not clear at all, where a '5' would mean the answer is crystal clear and defined. Leave emtpy when the question is not applicable or you don't want to answer it, you can skip it without affecting your score. Write your score in the space provided.

After you have responded to all the appropriate statements in each section, compute your average score for that section, using the formula provided, and round to the nearest tenth. Then transfer to the corresponding spoke in the Infrastructure Decisions Scorecard on the second next page of the Self-Assessment.

Your completed Infrastructure Decisions Scorecard will give you a clear presentation of which Infrastructure Decisions areas need attention.

Infrastructure Decisions Scorecard Example

Example of how the finalized Scorecard can look like:

Infrastructure Decisions Scorecard

Your Scores:

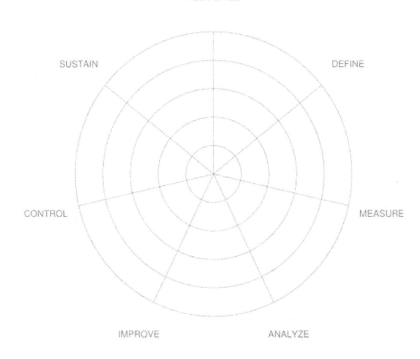

BEGINNING OF THE SELF-ASSESSMENT:

CRITERION #1: RECOGNIZE

INTENT: Be aware of the need for change. Recognize that there is an unfavorable variation, problem or symptom.

In my belief, the answer to this question is clearly defined:

5 Strongly Agree

4 Agree

3 Neutral

2 Disagree

1 Strongly Disagree

1. How does it fit into your organizational needs and tasks?
<--- Score

2. Are there recognized infrastructure decisions problems?
<--- Score

3. What are the clients issues and concerns?

<--- Score

4. How do you identify the kinds of information that you will need?
<--- Score

5. Is the quality assurance team identified?
<--- Score

6. What problems are you facing and how do you consider infrastructure decisions will circumvent those obstacles?
<--- Score

7. Do you know what you need to know about infrastructure decisions?
<--- Score

8. What infrastructure decisions problem should be solved?
<--- Score

9. What are the timeframes required to resolve each of the issues/problems?
<--- Score

10. Why the need?
<--- Score

11. What is the smallest subset of the problem you can usefully solve?
<--- Score

12. What is the extent or complexity of the infrastructure decisions problem?
<--- Score

13. What is the problem or issue?
<--- Score

14. Are you dealing with any of the same issues today as yesterday? What can you do about this?
<--- Score

15. What creative shifts do you need to take?
<--- Score

16. Do you need to avoid or amend any infrastructure decisions activities?
<--- Score

17. Have you identified your infrastructure decisions key performance indicators?
<--- Score

18. What tools and technologies are needed for a custom infrastructure decisions project?
<--- Score

19. What do employees need in the short term?
<--- Score

20. When a infrastructure decisions manager recognizes a problem, what options are available?
<--- Score

21. What are the stakeholder objectives to be achieved with infrastructure decisions?
<--- Score

22. What vendors make products that address the infrastructure decisions needs?

<--- Score

23. Do you need different information or graphics?
<--- Score

24. Are there any specific expectations or concerns about the infrastructure decisions team, infrastructure decisions itself?
<--- Score

25. Do you recognize infrastructure decisions achievements?
<--- Score

26. Will new equipment/products be required to facilitate infrastructure decisions delivery, for example is new software needed?
<--- Score

27. Is the need for organizational change recognized?
<--- Score

28. Which information does the infrastructure decisions business case need to include?
<--- Score

29. Who needs what information?
<--- Score

30. How do you recognize an objection?
<--- Score

31. Who needs to know about infrastructure decisions?
<--- Score

32. Consider your own infrastructure decisions project, what types of organizational problems do you think might be causing or affecting your problem, based on the work done so far?
<--- Score

33. Which issues are too important to ignore?
<--- Score

34. Think about the people you identified for your infrastructure decisions project and the project responsibilities you would assign to them, what kind of training do you think they would need to perform these responsibilities effectively?
<--- Score

35. Did you miss any major infrastructure decisions issues?
<--- Score

36. What activities does the governance board need to consider?
<--- Score

37. Who else hopes to benefit from it?
<--- Score

38. What would happen if infrastructure decisions weren't done?
<--- Score

39. How do you recognize an infrastructure decisions objection?
<--- Score

40. What do you need to start doing?

<--- Score

41. How many trainings, in total, are needed?
<--- Score

42. Are there any revenue recognition issues?
<--- Score

43. For your infrastructure decisions project, identify and describe the business environment, is there more than one layer to the business environment?
<--- Score

44. Are problem definition and motivation clearly presented?
<--- Score

45. How do you assess your infrastructure decisions workforce capability and capacity needs, including skills, competencies, and staffing levels?
<--- Score

46. Will a response program recognize when a crisis occurs and provide some level of response?
<--- Score

47. What infrastructure decisions events should you attend?
<--- Score

48. How do you identify subcontractor relationships?
<--- Score

49. What resources or support might you need?
<--- Score

50. What needs to stay?
<--- Score

51. Is it needed?
<--- Score

52. To what extent would your organization benefit from being recognized as a award recipient?
<--- Score

53. Where is training needed?
<--- Score

54. Are losses recognized in a timely manner?
<--- Score

55. Will infrastructure decisions deliverables need to be tested and, if so, by whom?
<--- Score

56. How much are sponsors, customers, partners, stakeholders involved in infrastructure decisions? In other words, what are the risks, if infrastructure decisions does not deliver successfully?
<--- Score

57. Will it solve real problems?
<--- Score

58. What is the infrastructure decisions problem definition? What do you need to resolve?
<--- Score

59. As a sponsor, customer or management, how important is it to meet goals, objectives?

<--- Score

60. How are you going to measure success?
<--- Score

61. Why is this needed?
<--- Score

62. Who defines the rules in relation to any given issue?
<--- Score

63. To what extent does each concerned units management team recognize infrastructure decisions as an effective investment?
<--- Score

64. Does the problem have ethical dimensions?
<--- Score

65. Are employees recognized or rewarded for performance that demonstrates the highest levels of integrity?
<--- Score

66. What infrastructure decisions capabilities do you need?
<--- Score

67. Would you recognize a threat from the inside?
<--- Score

68. What else needs to be measured?
<--- Score

69. Are there regulatory / compliance issues?

<--- Score

70. Who needs budgets?
<--- Score

71. Who should resolve the infrastructure decisions issues?
<--- Score

72. What are the expected benefits of infrastructure decisions to the stakeholder?
<--- Score

73. How are training requirements identified?
<--- Score

74. What infrastructure decisions coordination do you need?
<--- Score

75. Which needs are not included or involved?
<--- Score

76. What are the minority interests and what amount of minority interests can be recognized?
<--- Score

77. What is the problem and/or vulnerability?
<--- Score

78. What should be considered when identifying available resources, constraints, and deadlines?
<--- Score

79. What extra resources will you need?
<--- Score

80. Do you have/need 24-hour access to key personnel?
<--- Score

81. Are your goals realistic? Do you need to redefine your problem? Perhaps the problem has changed or maybe you have reached your goal and need to set a new one?
<--- Score

82. What are your needs in relation to infrastructure decisions skills, labor, equipment, and markets?
<--- Score

83. Who are your key stakeholders who need to sign off?
<--- Score

84. Looking at each person individually – does every one have the qualities which are needed to work in this group?
<--- Score

85. What needs to be done?
<--- Score

86. What prevents you from making the changes you know will make you a more effective infrastructure decisions leader?
<--- Score

87. What information do users need?
<--- Score

88. What is the recognized need?
<--- Score

89. Are employees recognized for desired behaviors?
<--- Score

90. Does infrastructure decisions create potential expectations in other areas that need to be recognized and considered?
<--- Score

91. What are the infrastructure decisions resources needed?
<--- Score

92. What situation(s) led to this infrastructure decisions Self Assessment?
<--- Score

93. Are there infrastructure decisions problems defined?
<--- Score

94. What does infrastructure decisions success mean to the stakeholders?
<--- Score

95. How can auditing be a preventative security measure?
<--- Score

96. Who needs to know?
<--- Score

97. Whom do you really need or want to serve?
<--- Score

98. How are the infrastructure decisions's objectives aligned to the group's overall stakeholder strategy?
<--- Score

99. Is it clear when you think of the day ahead of you what activities and tasks you need to complete?
<--- Score

100. How do you take a forward-looking perspective in identifying infrastructure decisions research related to market response and models?
<--- Score

101. Can management personnel recognize the monetary benefit of infrastructure decisions?
<--- Score

Add up total points for this section:
_ _ _ _ _ = Total points for this section

Divided by: _ _ _ _ _ _ (number of statements answered) = _ _ _ _ _ _
Average score for this section

Transfer your score to the infrastructure decisions Index at the beginning of the Self-Assessment.

CRITERION #2: DEFINE:

INTENT: Formulate the stakeholder problem. Define the problem, needs and objectives.

In my belief, the answer to this question is clearly defined:

5 Strongly Agree

4 Agree

3 Neutral

2 Disagree

1 Strongly Disagree

1. How are consistent infrastructure decisions definitions important?
<--- Score

2. Is it clearly defined in and to your organization what you do?
<--- Score

3. Have specific policy objectives been defined?

<--- Score

4. What information should you gather?
<--- Score

5. Is the improvement team aware of the different versions of a process: what they think it is vs. what it actually is vs. what it should be vs. what it could be?
<--- Score

6. How will variation in the actual durations of each activity be dealt with to ensure that the expected infrastructure decisions results are met?
<--- Score

7. If substitutes have been appointed, have they been briefed on the infrastructure decisions goals and received regular communications as to the progress to date?
<--- Score

8. What would be the goal or target for a infrastructure decisions's improvement team?
<--- Score

9. Have all basic functions of infrastructure decisions been defined?
<--- Score

10. How do you gather the stories?
<--- Score

11. How do you gather requirements?
<--- Score

12. What intelligence can you gather?

<--- Score

13. What is in the scope and what is not in scope?
<--- Score

14. What defines best in class?
<--- Score

15. Are task requirements clearly defined?
<--- Score

16. What is the scope of the infrastructure decisions effort?
<--- Score

17. What is the definition of infrastructure decisions excellence?
<--- Score

18. What is the scope?
<--- Score

19. Who is gathering infrastructure decisions information?
<--- Score

20. Has the direction changed at all during the course of infrastructure decisions? If so, when did it change and why?
<--- Score

21. What are the dynamics of the communication plan?
<--- Score

22. How was the 'as is' process map developed,

reviewed, verified and validated?
<--- Score

23. Is there any additional infrastructure decisions definition of success?
<--- Score

24. Is infrastructure decisions currently on schedule according to the plan?
<--- Score

25. The political context: who holds power?
<--- Score

26. How do you manage scope?
<--- Score

27. Is the current 'as is' process being followed? If not, what are the discrepancies?
<--- Score

28. Are different versions of process maps needed to account for the different types of inputs?
<--- Score

29. Who defines (or who defined) the rules and roles?
<--- Score

30. Is infrastructure decisions required?
<--- Score

31. What baselines are required to be defined and managed?
<--- Score

32. Does the team have regular meetings?
<--- Score

33. What scope to assess?
<--- Score

34. Has your scope been defined?
<--- Score

35. Are all requirements met?
<--- Score

36. What are the Roles and Responsibilities for each team member and its leadership? Where is this documented?
<--- Score

37. What happens if infrastructure decisions's scope changes?
<--- Score

38. Have the customer needs been translated into specific, measurable requirements? How?
<--- Score

39. Are customer(s) identified and segmented according to their different needs and requirements?
<--- Score

40. What gets examined?
<--- Score

41. What are the compelling stakeholder reasons for embarking on infrastructure decisions?
<--- Score

42. What are the boundaries of the scope? What is in bounds and what is not? What is the start point? What is the stop point?
<--- Score

43. How do you keep key subject matter experts in the loop?
<--- Score

44. How did the infrastructure decisions manager receive input to the development of a infrastructure decisions improvement plan and the estimated completion dates/times of each activity?
<--- Score

45. How have you defined all infrastructure decisions requirements first?
<--- Score

46. Is data collected and displayed to better understand customer(s) critical needs and requirements.
<--- Score

47. What scope do you want your strategy to cover?
<--- Score

48. In what way can you redefine the criteria of choice clients have in your category in your favor?
<--- Score

49. Has a team charter been developed and communicated?
<--- Score

50. How do you gather infrastructure decisions requirements?
<--- Score

51. Is the infrastructure decisions scope complete and appropriately sized?
<--- Score

52. Will a infrastructure decisions production readiness review be required?
<--- Score

53. Is special infrastructure decisions user knowledge required?
<--- Score

54. Do you have a infrastructure decisions success story or case study ready to tell and share?
<--- Score

55. Is scope creep really all bad news?
<--- Score

56. Are approval levels defined for contracts and supplements to contracts?
<--- Score

57. When is the estimated completion date?
<--- Score

58. How do you catch infrastructure decisions definition inconsistencies?
<--- Score

59. Is the scope of infrastructure decisions defined?

<--- Score

60. What are the infrastructure decisions use cases?

<--- Score

61. Is there regularly 100% attendance at the team meetings? If not, have appointed substitutes attended to preserve cross-functionality and full representation?

<--- Score

62. Are the infrastructure decisions requirements complete?

<--- Score

63. What are the core elements of the infrastructure decisions business case?

<--- Score

64. When is/was the infrastructure decisions start date?

<--- Score

65. Is infrastructure decisions linked to key stakeholder goals and objectives?

<--- Score

66. How is the team tracking and documenting its work?

<--- Score

67. Are roles and responsibilities formally defined?

<--- Score

68. What are the requirements for audit

information?
<--- Score

69. What infrastructure decisions services do you require?
<--- Score

70. How often are the team meetings?
<--- Score

71. Is there a infrastructure decisions management charter, including stakeholder case, problem and goal statements, scope, milestones, roles and responsibilities, communication plan?
<--- Score

72. What are the rough order estimates on cost savings/opportunities that infrastructure decisions brings?
<--- Score

73. How do you manage changes in infrastructure decisions requirements?
<--- Score

74. What sort of initial information to gather?
<--- Score

75. What is the context?
<--- Score

76. Has a project plan, Gantt chart, or similar been developed/completed?
<--- Score

77. Are there different segments of customers?

<--- Score

78. What information do you gather?
<--- Score

79. Is the team adequately staffed with the desired cross-functionality? If not, what additional resources are available to the team?
<--- Score

80. Are required metrics defined, what are they?
<--- Score

81. What customer feedback methods were used to solicit their input?
<--- Score

82. What are the record-keeping requirements of infrastructure decisions activities?
<--- Score

83. Has the infrastructure decisions work been fairly and/or equitably divided and delegated among team members who are qualified and capable to perform the work? Has everyone contributed?
<--- Score

84. Scope of sensitive information?
<--- Score

85. What constraints exist that might impact the team?
<--- Score

86. What is the worst case scenario?
<--- Score

87. How does the infrastructure decisions manager ensure against scope creep?
<--- Score

88. How do you hand over infrastructure decisions context?
<--- Score

89. What are (control) requirements for infrastructure decisions Information?
<--- Score

90. Is there a critical path to deliver infrastructure decisions results?
<--- Score

91. What is the scope of the infrastructure decisions work?
<--- Score

92. Has everyone on the team, including the team leaders, been properly trained?
<--- Score

93. Are audit criteria, scope, frequency and methods defined?
<--- Score

94. How do you think the partners involved in infrastructure decisions would have defined success?
<--- Score

95. Is there a completed SIPOC representation, describing the Suppliers, Inputs, Process, Outputs, and

Customers?

<--- Score

96. What critical content must be communicated –
who, what, when, where, and how?

<--- Score

97. How do you build the right business case?

<--- Score

98. How and when will the baselines be defined?

<--- Score

99. Do you all define infrastructure decisions in the
same way?

<--- Score

100. What infrastructure decisions requirements
should be gathered?

<--- Score

**101. Do you have organizational privacy
requirements?**

<--- Score

102. Who approved the infrastructure decisions
scope?

<--- Score

103. How would you define infrastructure decisions
leadership?

<--- Score

104. How would you define the culture at your
organization, how susceptible is it to infrastructure
decisions changes?

<--- Score

105. What system do you use for gathering infrastructure decisions information?
<--- Score

106. Why are you doing infrastructure decisions and what is the scope?
<--- Score

107. Are there any constraints known that bear on the ability to perform infrastructure decisions work? How is the team addressing them?
<--- Score

108. What specifically is the problem? Where does it occur? When does it occur? What is its extent?
<--- Score

109. Who are the infrastructure decisions improvement team members, including Management Leads and Coaches?
<--- Score

110. Are accountability and ownership for infrastructure decisions clearly defined?
<--- Score

111. What is in scope?
<--- Score

112. When are meeting minutes sent out? Who is on the distribution list?
<--- Score

113. Has a high-level 'as is' process map been

completed, verified and validated?
<--- Score

114. Are resources adequate for the scope?
<--- Score

115. Where can you gather more information?
<--- Score

116. Has/have the customer(s) been identified?
<--- Score

117. What are the infrastructure decisions tasks and definitions?
<--- Score

118. Has anyone else (internal or external to the group) attempted to solve this problem or a similar one before? If so, what knowledge can be leveraged from these previous efforts?
<--- Score

119. Has a infrastructure decisions requirement not been met?
<--- Score

120. Do the problem and goal statements meet the SMART criteria (specific, measurable, attainable, relevant, and time-bound)?
<--- Score

121. Has the improvement team collected the 'voice of the customer' (obtained feedback – qualitative and quantitative)?
<--- Score

122. What sources do you use to gather information for a infrastructure decisions study?
<--- Score

123. Is the infrastructure decisions scope manageable?
<--- Score

124. Have all of the relationships been defined properly?
<--- Score

125. Are the infrastructure decisions requirements testable?
<--- Score

126. What are the tasks and definitions?
<--- Score

127. Is there a completed, verified, and validated high-level 'as is' (not 'should be' or 'could be') stakeholder process map?
<--- Score

128. What is out-of-scope initially?
<--- Score

129. What is the definition of success?
<--- Score

130. How will the infrastructure decisions team and the group measure complete success of infrastructure decisions?
<--- Score

131. How can the value of infrastructure decisions be

defined?

<--- Score

132. What is out of scope?

<--- Score

133. What key stakeholder process output measure(s) does infrastructure decisions leverage and how?

<--- Score

134. How do you manage unclear infrastructure decisions requirements?

<--- Score

135. What is a worst-case scenario for losses?

<--- Score

136. Is the team equipped with available and reliable resources?

<--- Score

Add up total points for this section:
_ _ _ _ _ = Total points for this section

Divided by: _ _ _ _ _ _ (number of statements answered) = _ _ _ _ _ _
Average score for this section

Transfer your score to the infrastructure decisions Index at the beginning of the Self-Assessment.

CRITERION #3: MEASURE:

INTENT: Gather the correct data.
Measure the current performance and
evolution of the situation.

In my belief, the answer to this
question is clearly defined:

5 Strongly Agree

4 Agree

3 Neutral

2 Disagree

1 Strongly Disagree

1. How do you verify infrastructure decisions
completeness and accuracy?
<--- Score

2. Is it possible to estimate the impact of
unanticipated complexity such as wrong or failed
assumptions, feedback, etcetera on proposed
reforms?
<--- Score

3. Have you included everything in your infrastructure decisions cost models?
<--- Score

4. Is there an opportunity to verify requirements?
<--- Score

5. Are you able to realize any cost savings?
<--- Score

6. Do you verify that corrective actions were taken?
<--- Score

7. When are costs are incurred?
<--- Score

8. What are the costs of delaying infrastructure decisions action?
<--- Score

9. How will success or failure be measured?
<--- Score

10. How will costs be allocated?
<--- Score

11. Do you aggressively reward and promote the people who have the biggest impact on creating excellent infrastructure decisions services/products?
<--- Score

12. How will you measure your infrastructure decisions effectiveness?
<--- Score

13. What methods are feasible and acceptable to estimate the impact of reforms?
<--- Score

14. How can you manage cost down?
<--- Score

15. How long to keep data and how to manage retention costs?
<--- Score

16. What does verifying compliance entail?
<--- Score

17. How is the value delivered by infrastructure decisions being measured?
<--- Score

18. Do you have an issue in getting priority?
<--- Score

19. How can you reduce costs?
<--- Score

20. Which infrastructure decisions impacts are significant?
<--- Score

21. How can you reduce the costs of obtaining inputs?
<--- Score

22. What evidence is there and what is measured?
<--- Score

23. When a disaster occurs, who gets priority?

<--- Score

24. What is the infrastructure decisions business impact?
<--- Score

25. How do you verify and develop ideas and innovations?
<--- Score

26. What causes extra work or rework?
<--- Score

27. Are you taking your company in the direction of better and revenue or cheaper and cost?
<--- Score

28. Does management have the right priorities among projects?
<--- Score

29. What are your primary costs, revenues, assets?
<--- Score

30. How do you verify your resources?
<--- Score

31. What does a Test Case verify?
<--- Score

32. How do you measure variability?
<--- Score

33. When should you bother with diagrams?
<--- Score

34. How do you measure lifecycle phases?
<--- Score

35. What would it cost to replace your technology?
<--- Score

36. Who should receive measurement reports?
<--- Score

37. What causes investor action?
<--- Score

**38. What are hidden infrastructure decisions
quality costs?**
<--- Score

39. What is an unallowable cost?
<--- Score

40. Where is the cost?
<--- Score

41. Are the measurements objective?
<--- Score

42. What do you measure and why?
<--- Score

43. What disadvantage does this cause for the user?
<--- Score

44. What potential environmental factors impact the
infrastructure decisions effort?
<--- Score

45. How is progress measured?

<--- Score

46. Who pays the cost?
<--- Score

47. How are you verifying it?
<--- Score

48. Why do you expend time and effort to implement measurement, for whom?
<--- Score

49. What is the total cost related to deploying infrastructure decisions, including any consulting or professional services?
<--- Score

50. What tests verify requirements?
<--- Score

51. How will you measure success?
<--- Score

52. What does losing customers cost your organization?
<--- Score

53. What measurements are possible, practicable and meaningful?
<--- Score

54. How can a infrastructure decisions test verify your ideas or assumptions?
<--- Score

55. Are you aware of what could cause a problem?

<--- Score

56. Do you have a flow diagram of what happens?
<--- Score

57. Where can you go to verify the info?
<--- Score

58. What is the root cause(s) of the problem?
<--- Score

59. What happens if cost savings do not materialize?
<--- Score

60. How sensitive must the infrastructure decisions strategy be to cost?
<--- Score

61. What are allowable costs?
<--- Score

62. What details are required of the infrastructure decisions cost structure?
<--- Score

63. How are costs allocated?
<--- Score

64. How do your measurements capture actionable infrastructure decisions information for use in exceeding your customers expectations and securing your customers engagement?
<--- Score

65. What causes mismanagement?

<--- Score

66. What are the operational costs after infrastructure decisions deployment?
<--- Score

67. Do you effectively measure and reward individual and team performance?
<--- Score

68. How do you control the overall costs of your work processes?
<--- Score

69. Are infrastructure decisions vulnerabilities categorized and prioritized?
<--- Score

70. Are the units of measure consistent?
<--- Score

71. How can you measure infrastructure decisions in a systematic way?
<--- Score

72. What are your operating costs?
<--- Score

73. How do you verify if infrastructure decisions is built right?
<--- Score

74. Do the benefits outweigh the costs?
<--- Score

75. Are there any easy-to-implement alternatives

to infrastructure decisions? Sometimes other solutions are available that do not require the cost implications of a full-blown project?
<--- Score

76. What are the costs?
<--- Score

77. How do you measure success?
<--- Score

78. What is the cause of any infrastructure decisions gaps?
<--- Score

79. Why a infrastructure decisions focus?
<--- Score

80. What are the current costs of the infrastructure decisions process?
<--- Score

81. What does your operating model cost?
<--- Score

82. What are you verifying?
<--- Score

83. How much does it cost?
<--- Score

84. What are the infrastructure decisions key cost drivers?
<--- Score

85. Did you tackle the cause or the symptom?

<--- Score

86. What drives O&M cost?
<--- Score

87. Are actual costs in line with budgeted costs?
<--- Score

88. Are supply costs steady or fluctuating?
<--- Score

89. Does the infrastructure decisions task fit the client's priorities?
<--- Score

90. What are the uncertainties surrounding estimates of impact?
<--- Score

91. Have design-to-cost goals been established?
<--- Score

92. Are missed infrastructure decisions opportunities costing your organization money?
<--- Score

93. Are there measurements based on task performance?
<--- Score

94. What measurements are being captured?
<--- Score

95. How to cause the change?
<--- Score

96. What is the total fixed cost?
<--- Score

97. What could cause you to change course?
<--- Score

98. What are your customers expectations and measures?
<--- Score

99. Is the cost worth the infrastructure decisions effort ?
<--- Score

100. Which costs should be taken into account?
<--- Score

101. What are the strategic priorities for this year?
<--- Score

102. What is measured? Why?
<--- Score

103. What are the infrastructure decisions investment costs?
<--- Score

104. What do people want to verify?
<--- Score

105. How are measurements made?
<--- Score

106. How will effects be measured?
<--- Score

107. How frequently do you verify your infrastructure decisions strategy?
<--- Score

108. At what cost?
<--- Score

109. Will infrastructure decisions have an impact on current business continuity, disaster recovery processes and/or infrastructure?
<--- Score

110. How can you measure the performance?
<--- Score

111. What would be a real cause for concern?
<--- Score

112. How do you measure efficient delivery of infrastructure decisions services?
<--- Score

113. How do you prevent mis-estimating cost?
<--- Score

114. What are your key infrastructure decisions organizational performance measures, including key short and longer-term financial measures?
<--- Score

115. What are the types and number of measures to use?
<--- Score

116. How will measures be used to manage and adapt?

<--- Score

117. Has a cost center been established?
<--- Score

118. Do you have any cost infrastructure decisions limitation requirements?
<--- Score

119. What is your infrastructure decisions quality cost segregation study?
<--- Score

120. How do you verify the authenticity of the data and information used?
<--- Score

121. How do you verify performance?
<--- Score

122. What causes innovation to fail or succeed in your organization?
<--- Score

123. What could cause delays in the schedule?
<--- Score

124. How is performance measured?
<--- Score

125. Why do the measurements/indicators matter?
<--- Score

126. What relevant entities could be measured?
<--- Score

127. Does a infrastructure decisions quantification method exist?
<--- Score

128. Among the infrastructure decisions product and service cost to be estimated, which is considered hardest to estimate?
<--- Score

129. Are the infrastructure decisions benefits worth its costs?
<--- Score

130. What is your decision requirements diagram?
<--- Score

131. How do you verify and validate the infrastructure decisions data?
<--- Score

132. Which measures and indicators matter?
<--- Score

133. Is the solution cost-effective?
<--- Score

134. How will your organization measure success?
<--- Score

135. How frequently do you track infrastructure decisions measures?
<--- Score

136. How do you quantify and qualify impacts?
<--- Score

137. What are the costs of reform?
<--- Score

Add up total points for this section:
_____ = Total points for this section

Divided by: _____ (number of
statements answered) = _____
Average score for this section

Transfer your score to the infrastructure
decisions Index at the beginning of the
Self-Assessment.

CRITERION #4: ANALYZE:

INTENT: Analyze causes, assumptions and hypotheses.

In my belief, the answer to this question is clearly defined:

5 Strongly Agree

4 Agree

3 Neutral

2 Disagree

1 Strongly Disagree

1. How much data can be collected in the given timeframe?
<--- Score

2. What are the processes for audit reporting and management?
<--- Score

3. Is the required infrastructure decisions data gathered?

<--- Score

4. How was the detailed process map generated, verified, and validated?
<--- Score

5. How is the way you as the leader think and process information affecting your organizational culture?
<--- Score

6. Do your contracts/agreements contain data security obligations?
<--- Score

7. What are the infrastructure decisions design outputs?
<--- Score

8. Did any additional data need to be collected?
<--- Score

9. How does the organization define, manage, and improve its infrastructure decisions processes?
<--- Score

10. Do your employees have the opportunity to do what they do best everyday?
<--- Score

11. How is the infrastructure decisions Value Stream Mapping managed?
<--- Score

12. How do you measure the operational performance of your key work systems and processes, including

productivity, cycle time, and other appropriate measures of process effectiveness, efficiency, and innovation?
<--- Score

13. What process should you select for improvement?
<--- Score

14. Who will gather what data?
<--- Score

15. Who will facilitate the team and process?
<--- Score

16. Think about some of the processes you undertake within your organization, which do you own?
<--- Score

17. What is the infrastructure decisions Driver?
<--- Score

18. What were the crucial 'moments of truth' on the process map?
<--- Score

19. What types of data do your infrastructure decisions indicators require?
<--- Score

20. How will the change process be managed?
<--- Score

21. Did any value-added analysis or 'lean thinking' take place to identify some of the gaps shown on the 'as is' process map?
<--- Score

22. Are gaps between current performance and the goal performance identified?
<--- Score

23. How is infrastructure decisions data gathered?
<--- Score

24. What qualifications are necessary?
<--- Score

25. What did the team gain from developing a sub-process map?
<--- Score

26. Was a detailed process map created to amplify critical steps of the 'as is' stakeholder process?
<--- Score

27. What infrastructure decisions metrics are outputs of the process?
<--- Score

28. How do you implement and manage your work processes to ensure that they meet design requirements?
<--- Score

29. Was a cause-and-effect diagram used to explore the different types of causes (or sources of variation)?
<--- Score

30. What is your organizations process which leads to recognition of value generation?
<--- Score

31. Do several people in different organizational units assist with the infrastructure decisions process?
<--- Score

32. What other organizational variables, such as reward systems or communication systems, affect the performance of this infrastructure decisions process?
<--- Score

33. What controls do you have in place to protect data?
<--- Score

34. What, related to, infrastructure decisions processes does your organization outsource?
<--- Score

35. Do staff qualifications match your project?
<--- Score

36. What is your organizations system for selecting qualified vendors?
<--- Score

37. Who qualifies to gain access to data?
<--- Score

38. What kind of crime could a potential new hire have committed that would not only not disqualify him/her from being hired by your organization, but would actually indicate that he/she might be a particularly good fit?
<--- Score

39. What qualifications do infrastructure decisions leaders need?

<--- Score

40. What are the necessary qualifications?

<--- Score

41. Have any additional benefits been identified that will result from closing all or most of the gaps?

<--- Score

42. What is the Value Stream Mapping?

<--- Score

43. What tools were used to narrow the list of possible causes?

<--- Score

44. What is the output?

<--- Score

45. Have the problem and goal statements been updated to reflect the additional knowledge gained from the analyze phase?

<--- Score

46. Is the gap/opportunity displayed and communicated in financial terms?

<--- Score

47. Do quality systems drive continuous improvement?

<--- Score

48. What are the personnel training and qualifications required?

<--- Score

49. What successful thing are you doing today that may be blinding you to new growth opportunities?
<--- Score

50. What internal processes need improvement?
<--- Score

51. What is the cost of poor quality as supported by the team's analysis?
<--- Score

52. Where can you get qualified talent today?
<--- Score

53. What tools were used to generate the list of possible causes?
<--- Score

54. What other jobs or tasks affect the performance of the steps in the infrastructure decisions process?
<--- Score

55. What training and qualifications will you need?
<--- Score

56. What will drive infrastructure decisions change?
<--- Score

57. How will the infrastructure decisions data be captured?
<--- Score

58. Are all staff in core infrastructure decisions subjects Highly Qualified?

<--- Score

59. Which infrastructure decisions data should be retained?
<--- Score

60. Who is involved in the management review process?
<--- Score

61. Who is involved with workflow mapping?
<--- Score

62. How do you identify specific infrastructure decisions investment opportunities and emerging trends?
<--- Score

63. Is the final output clearly identified?
<--- Score

64. What does the data say about the performance of the stakeholder process?
<--- Score

65. How difficult is it to qualify what infrastructure decisions ROI is?
<--- Score

66. Has data output been validated?
<--- Score

67. Were Pareto charts (or similar) used to portray the 'heavy hitters' (or key sources of variation)?
<--- Score

68. What is the complexity of the output produced?
<--- Score

69. Are you missing infrastructure decisions opportunities?
<--- Score

70. Are infrastructure decisions changes recognized early enough to be approved through the regular process?
<--- Score

71. What infrastructure decisions data will be collected?
<--- Score

72. What qualifies as competition?
<--- Score

73. Where is the data coming from to measure compliance?
<--- Score

74. What are your infrastructure decisions processes?
<--- Score

75. What systems/processes must you excel at?
<--- Score

76. What infrastructure decisions data should be collected?
<--- Score

77. What are your key performance measures or indicators and in-process measures for the control

and improvement of your infrastructure decisions processes?
<--- Score

78. What quality tools were used to get through the analyze phase?
<--- Score

79. How has the infrastructure decisions data been gathered?
<--- Score

80. Is there a strict change management process?
<--- Score

81. How will corresponding data be collected?
<--- Score

82. Is data and process analysis, root cause analysis and quantifying the gap/opportunity in place?
<--- Score

83. How do you promote understanding that opportunity for improvement is not criticism of the status quo, or the people who created the status quo?
<--- Score

84. What data is gathered?
<--- Score

85. Is pre-qualification of suppliers carried out?
<--- Score

86. Is the performance gap determined?
<--- Score

87. Can you add value to the current infrastructure decisions decision-making process (largely qualitative) by incorporating uncertainty modeling (more quantitative)?
<--- Score

88. What are the best opportunities for value improvement?
<--- Score

89. What infrastructure decisions data should be managed?
<--- Score

90. Is there an established change management process?
<--- Score

91. Are all team members qualified for all tasks?
<--- Score

92. What process improvements will be needed?
<--- Score

93. When should a process be art not science?
<--- Score

94. Are your outputs consistent?
<--- Score

95. How do you ensure that the infrastructure decisions opportunity is realistic?
<--- Score

96. How will the data be checked for quality?
<--- Score

97. Do you, as a leader, bounce back quickly from setbacks?
<--- Score

98. How do you define collaboration and team output?
<--- Score

99. An organizationally feasible system request is one that considers the mission, goals and objectives of the organization, key questions are: is the infrastructure decisions solution request practical and will it solve a problem or take advantage of an opportunity to achieve company goals?
<--- Score

100. How can risk management be tied procedurally to process elements?
<--- Score

101. Have you defined which data is gathered how?
<--- Score

102. What output to create?
<--- Score

103. Record-keeping requirements flow from the records needed as inputs, outputs, controls and for transformation of a infrastructure decisions process, are the records needed as inputs to the infrastructure decisions process available?
<--- Score

104. What are your outputs?
<--- Score

105. Were any designed experiments used to generate additional insight into the data analysis?
<--- Score

106. What were the financial benefits resulting from any 'ground fruit or low-hanging fruit' (quick fixes)?
<--- Score

107. Do you understand your management processes today?
<--- Score

108. What are your current levels and trends in key measures or indicators of infrastructure decisions product and process performance that are important to and directly serve your customers? How do these results compare with the performance of your competitors and other organizations with similar offerings?
<--- Score

109. How are outputs preserved and protected?
<--- Score

110. How do you use infrastructure decisions data and information to support organizational decision making and innovation?
<--- Score

111. What resources go in to get the desired output?
<--- Score

112. What is the oversight process?
<--- Score

113. How is data used for program management and improvement?

<--- Score

114. What are your current levels and trends in key infrastructure decisions measures or indicators of product and process performance that are important to and directly serve your customers?

<--- Score

115. What qualifications and skills do you need?

<--- Score

116. What do you need to qualify?

<--- Score

117. Is the infrastructure decisions process severely broken such that a re-design is necessary?

<--- Score

118. Who gets your output?

<--- Score

119. What qualifications are needed?

<--- Score

120. What are your best practices for minimizing infrastructure decisions project risk, while demonstrating incremental value and quick wins throughout the infrastructure decisions project lifecycle?

<--- Score

121. How many input/output points does it require?

<--- Score

122. Where is infrastructure decisions data gathered?
<--- Score

123. How do your work systems and key work processes relate to and capitalize on your core competencies?
<--- Score

124. Identify an operational issue in your organization, for example, could a particular task be done more quickly or more efficiently by infrastructure decisions?
<--- Score

125. What conclusions were drawn from the team's data collection and analysis? How did the team reach these conclusions?
<--- Score

126. Is the suppliers process defined and controlled?
<--- Score

127. Were there any improvement opportunities identified from the process analysis?
<--- Score

128. Should you invest in industry-recognized qualifications?
<--- Score

129. How is the data gathered?
<--- Score

130. What information qualified as important?
<--- Score

131. What are the revised rough estimates of the

financial savings/opportunity for infrastructure decisions improvements?

<--- Score

132. Who owns what data?

<--- Score

133. Has an output goal been set?

<--- Score

134. Think about the functions involved in your infrastructure decisions project, what processes flow from these functions?

<--- Score

135. Do your leaders quickly bounce back from setbacks?

<--- Score

Add up total points for this section:
_ _ _ _ _ = Total points for this section

Divided by: _ _ _ _ _ _ (number of statements answered) = _ _ _ _ _ _
Average score for this section

Transfer your score to the infrastructure decisions Index at the beginning of the Self-Assessment.

CRITERION #5: IMPROVE:

INTENT: Develop a practical solution. Innovate, establish and test the solution and to measure the results.

In my belief, the answer to this question is clearly defined:

5 Strongly Agree

4 Agree

3 Neutral

2 Disagree

1 Strongly Disagree

1. What is infrastructure decisions risk?
<--- Score

2. Can you identify any significant risks or exposures to infrastructure decisions third- parties (vendors, service providers, alliance partners etc) that concern you?
<--- Score

3. How will you know that a change is an improvement?
<--- Score

4. Who makes the infrastructure decisions decisions in your organization?
<--- Score

5. How are policy decisions made and where?
<--- Score

6. For decision problems, how do you develop a decision statement?
<--- Score

7. What tools do you use once you have decided on a infrastructure decisions strategy and more importantly how do you choose?
<--- Score

8. Who controls key decisions that will be made?
<--- Score

9. What alternative responses are available to manage risk?
<--- Score

10. How risky is your organization?
<--- Score

11. Are procedures documented for managing infrastructure decisions risks?
<--- Score

12. Does the goal represent a desired result that can be measured?

<--- Score

13. What practices helps your organization to develop its capacity to recognize patterns?
<--- Score

14. How scalable is your infrastructure decisions solution?
<--- Score

15. Is the measure of success for infrastructure decisions understandable to a variety of people?
<--- Score

16. How can skill-level changes improve infrastructure decisions?
<--- Score

17. In the past few months, what is the smallest change you have made that has had the biggest positive result? What was it about that small change that produced the large return?
<--- Score

18. If you could go back in time five years, what decision would you make differently? What is your best guess as to what decision you're making today you might regret five years from now?
<--- Score

19. When you map the key players in your own work and the types/domains of relationships with them, which relationships do you find easy and which challenging, and why?
<--- Score

20. What to do with the results or outcomes of measurements?
<--- Score

21. What tools were used to tap into the creativity and encourage 'outside the box' thinking?
<--- Score

22. How do you deal with infrastructure decisions risk?
<--- Score

23. What can you do to improve?
<--- Score

24. Who will be responsible for documenting the infrastructure decisions requirements in detail?
<--- Score

25. How do you mitigate infrastructure decisions risk?
<--- Score

26. Are risk triggers captured?
<--- Score

27. Who controls the risk?
<--- Score

28. What current systems have to be understood and/ or changed?
<--- Score

29. Was a infrastructure decisions charter developed?
<--- Score

30. How do you improve productivity?
<--- Score

31. What improvements have been achieved?
<--- Score

32. Do those selected for the infrastructure decisions team have a good general understanding of what infrastructure decisions is all about?
<--- Score

33. What area needs the greatest improvement?
<--- Score

34. What risks do you need to manage?
<--- Score

35. What error proofing will be done to address some of the discrepancies observed in the 'as is' process?
<--- Score

36. Would you develop a infrastructure decisions Communication Strategy?
<--- Score

37. Is infrastructure decisions documentation maintained?
<--- Score

38. How do you measure progress and evaluate training effectiveness?
<--- Score

39. What lessons, if any, from a pilot were incorporated into the design of the full-scale solution?
<--- Score

40. What is the team's contingency plan for potential

problems occurring in implementation?

<--- Score

41. How can the phases of infrastructure decisions development be identified?

<--- Score

42. Who are the infrastructure decisions decision makers?

<--- Score

43. What is infrastructure decisions's impact on utilizing the best solution(s)?

<--- Score

44. Which of the recognised risks out of all risks can be most likely transferred?

<--- Score

45. What attendant changes will need to be made to ensure that the solution is successful?

<--- Score

46. Who are the infrastructure decisions decision-makers?

<--- Score

47. Is supporting infrastructure decisions documentation required?

<--- Score

48. Who do you report infrastructure decisions results to?

<--- Score

49. How are infrastructure decisions risks managed?

<--- Score

50. Will the controls trigger any other risks?
<--- Score

51. To what extent does management recognize infrastructure decisions as a tool to increase the results?
<--- Score

52. Was a pilot designed for the proposed solution(s)?
<--- Score

53. Are the risks fully understood, reasonable and manageable?
<--- Score

54. Risk events: what are the things that could go wrong?
<--- Score

55. What are the implications of the one critical infrastructure decisions decision 10 minutes, 10 months, and 10 years from now?
<--- Score

56. Can the solution be designed and implemented within an acceptable time period?
<--- Score

57. How do you improve infrastructure decisions service perception, and satisfaction?
<--- Score

58. What are the concrete infrastructure decisions results?

<--- Score

59. What tools were used to evaluate the potential solutions?
<--- Score

60. What should a proof of concept or pilot accomplish?
<--- Score

61. What actually has to improve and by how much?
<--- Score

62. Explorations of the frontiers of infrastructure decisions will help you build influence, improve infrastructure decisions, optimize decision making, and sustain change, what is your approach?
<--- Score

63. What does the 'should be' process map/design look like?
<--- Score

64. What resources are required for the improvement efforts?
<--- Score

65. Who are the people involved in developing and implementing infrastructure decisions?
<--- Score

66. Who will be using the results of the measurement activities?
<--- Score

67. How will you know when its improved?
<--- Score

68. Is the infrastructure decisions documentation thorough?
<--- Score

69. What is the implementation plan?
<--- Score

70. What are your current levels and trends in key measures or indicators of workforce and leader development?
<--- Score

71. Why improve in the first place?
<--- Score

72. Risk Identification: What are the possible risk events your organization faces in relation to infrastructure decisions?
<--- Score

73. Is the infrastructure decisions risk managed?
<--- Score

74. Have you identified breakpoints and/or risk tolerances that will trigger broad consideration of a potential need for intervention or modification of strategy?
<--- Score

75. Is risk periodically assessed?
<--- Score

76. Do vendor agreements bring new compliance risk

?
<--- Score

77. How do you improve your likelihood of success ?
<--- Score

78. How will you recognize and celebrate results?
<--- Score

79. How do you manage and improve your
infrastructure decisions work systems to deliver
customer value and achieve organizational success
and sustainability?
<--- Score

80. Is there a high likelihood that any
recommendations will achieve their intended results?
<--- Score

81. How does your organization evaluate strategic
infrastructure decisions success?
<--- Score

82. Who are the key stakeholders for the infrastructure
decisions evaluation?
<--- Score

83. Were any criteria developed to assist the team in
testing and evaluating potential solutions?
<--- Score

84. What tools were most useful during the improve
phase?
<--- Score

85. What were the underlying assumptions on the

cost-benefit analysis?
<--- Score

86. Do you have the optimal project management team structure?
<--- Score

87. Are decisions made in a timely manner?
<--- Score

88. What strategies for infrastructure decisions improvement are successful?
<--- Score

89. For estimation problems, how do you develop an estimation statement?
<--- Score

90. How significant is the improvement in the eyes of the end user?
<--- Score

91. Is the solution technically practical?
<--- Score

92. What is the infrastructure decisions's sustainability risk?
<--- Score

93. Are the key business and technology risks being managed?
<--- Score

94. Risk factors: what are the characteristics of infrastructure decisions that make it risky?
<--- Score

95. Do you cover the five essential competencies: Communication, Collaboration,Innovation, Adaptability, and Leadership that improve an organizations ability to leverage the new infrastructure decisions in a volatile global economy?

<--- Score

96. How do you measure improved infrastructure decisions service perception, and satisfaction?

<--- Score

97. Are you assessing infrastructure decisions and risk?

<--- Score

98. Where do the infrastructure decisions decisions reside?

<--- Score

99. How do you decide how much to remunerate an employee?

<--- Score

100. How will you measure the results?

<--- Score

101. How do you measure risk?

<--- Score

102. How do you link measurement and risk?

<--- Score

103. Do you combine technical expertise with business knowledge and infrastructure decisions Key

topics include lifecycles, development approaches, requirements and how to make a business case?
<--- Score

104. Can you integrate quality management and risk management?
<--- Score

105. Are events managed to resolution?
<--- Score

106. Do you need to do a usability evaluation?
<--- Score

107. How do you define the solutions' scope?
<--- Score

108. How is continuous improvement applied to risk management?
<--- Score

109. What are the expected infrastructure decisions results?
<--- Score

110. What went well, what should change, what can improve?
<--- Score

111. How can you better manage risk?
<--- Score

112. How do you keep improving infrastructure decisions?
<--- Score

113. How will you know that you have improved?
<--- Score

114. What criteria will you use to assess your infrastructure decisions risks?
<--- Score

115. How do you go about comparing infrastructure decisions approaches/solutions?
<--- Score

116. What needs improvement? Why?
<--- Score

117. Is any infrastructure decisions documentation required?
<--- Score

118. How risky is your organization?
<--- Score

119. How do you manage infrastructure decisions risk?
<--- Score

120. How does the team improve its work?
<--- Score

121. How do the infrastructure decisions results compare with the performance of your competitors and other organizations with similar offerings?
<--- Score

122. Is there a small-scale pilot for proposed improvement(s)? What conclusions were drawn from the outcomes of a pilot?

<--- Score

123. Is there any other infrastructure decisions solution?
<--- Score

124. What communications are necessary to support the implementation of the solution?
<--- Score

125. infrastructure decisions risk decisions: whose call Is It?
<--- Score

126. How can you improve performance?
<--- Score

127. Does a good decision guarantee a good outcome?
<--- Score

128. Is the scope clearly documented?
<--- Score

129. Have you achieved infrastructure decisions improvements?
<--- Score

Add up total points for this section:
_ _ _ _ _ = Total points for this section

Divided by: _ _ _ _ _ _ (number of statements answered) = _ _ _ _ _ _ Average score for this section

Transfer your score to the infrastructure

decisions Index at the beginning of the
Self-Assessment.

CRITERION #6: CONTROL:

INTENT: Implement the practical solution. Maintain the performance and correct possible complications.

In my belief, the answer to this question is clearly defined:

5 Strongly Agree

4 Agree

3 Neutral

2 Disagree

1 Strongly Disagree

1. Have new or revised work instructions resulted?
<--- Score

2. What are your results for key measures or indicators of the accomplishment of your infrastructure decisions strategy and action plans, including building and strengthening core competencies?
<--- Score

3. How will the process owner and team be able to hold the gains?
<--- Score

4. What is the control/monitoring plan?
<--- Score

5. Does job training on the documented procedures need to be part of the process team's education and training?
<--- Score

6. Is there a documented and implemented monitoring plan?
<--- Score

7. Are operating procedures consistent?
<--- Score

8. What are the critical parameters to watch?
<--- Score

9. What are the known security controls?
<--- Score

10. What is the recommended frequency of auditing?
<--- Score

11. What is your theory of human motivation, and how does your compensation plan fit with that view?
<--- Score

12. What are the key elements of your infrastructure decisions performance improvement system, including your evaluation, organizational learning, and innovation processes?

<--- Score

13. Is there a control plan in place for sustaining improvements (short and long-term)?
<--- Score

14. How do you plan for the cost of succession?
<--- Score

15. Does the response plan contain a definite closed loop continual improvement scheme (e.g., plan-do-check-act)?
<--- Score

16. Are suggested corrective/restorative actions indicated on the response plan for known causes to problems that might surface?
<--- Score

17. What key inputs and outputs are being measured on an ongoing basis?
<--- Score

18. What other areas of the group might benefit from the infrastructure decisions team's improvements, knowledge, and learning?
<--- Score

19. Do the infrastructure decisions decisions you make today help people and the planet tomorrow?
<--- Score

20. Can you adapt and adjust to changing infrastructure decisions situations?
<--- Score

21. How do you establish and deploy modified action plans if circumstances require a shift in plans and rapid execution of new plans?
<--- Score

22. Are there documented procedures?
<--- Score

23. What do you stand for--and what are you against?
<--- Score

24. What do you measure to verify effectiveness gains?
<--- Score

25. Can support from partners be adjusted?
<--- Score

26. Where do ideas that reach policy makers and planners as proposals for infrastructure decisions strengthening and reform actually originate?
<--- Score

27. How will report readings be checked to effectively monitor performance?
<--- Score

28. Is a response plan established and deployed?
<--- Score

29. Are the infrastructure decisions standards challenging?
<--- Score

30. Are you measuring, monitoring and predicting infrastructure decisions activities to optimize

operations and profitability, and enhancing outcomes?

<--- Score

31. Does infrastructure decisions appropriately measure and monitor risk?

<--- Score

32. What adjustments to the strategies are needed?

<--- Score

33. How widespread is its use?

<--- Score

34. How will the day-to-day responsibilities for monitoring and continual improvement be transferred from the improvement team to the process owner?

<--- Score

35. Are the planned controls in place?

<--- Score

36. How do your controls stack up?

<--- Score

37. How do you monitor usage and cost?

<--- Score

38. Does a troubleshooting guide exist or is it needed?

<--- Score

39. Are the planned controls working?

<--- Score

40. Who sets the infrastructure decisions standards?

<--- Score

41. Will any special training be provided for results interpretation?

<--- Score

42. You may have created your quality measures at a time when you lacked resources, technology wasn't up to the required standard, or low service levels were the industry norm. Have those circumstances changed?

<--- Score

43. What can you control?

<--- Score

44. Is reporting being used or needed?

<--- Score

45. Is a response plan in place for when the input, process, or output measures indicate an 'out-of-control' condition?

<--- Score

46. How do senior leaders actions reflect a commitment to the organizations infrastructure decisions values?

<--- Score

47. How likely is the current infrastructure decisions plan to come in on schedule or on budget?

<--- Score

48. What other systems, operations, processes, and

infrastructures (hiring practices, staffing, training, incentives/rewards, metrics/dashboards/scorecards, etc.) need updates, additions, changes, or deletions in order to facilitate knowledge transfer and improvements?

<--- Score

49. Are controls in place and consistently applied?

<--- Score

50. Is there a recommended audit plan for routine surveillance inspections of infrastructure decisions's gains?

<--- Score

51. Against what alternative is success being measured?

<--- Score

52. Act/Adjust: What Do you Need to Do Differently?

<--- Score

53. Who controls critical resources?

<--- Score

54. Will the team be available to assist members in planning investigations?

<--- Score

55. Is there a standardized process?

<--- Score

56. How will input, process, and output variables be checked to detect for sub-optimal conditions?

<--- Score

57. Who has control over resources?

<--- Score

58. Is there an action plan in case of emergencies?

<--- Score

59. Has the infrastructure decisions value of standards been quantified?

<--- Score

60. How might the group capture best practices and lessons learned so as to leverage improvements?

<--- Score

61. How will the process owner verify improvement in present and future sigma levels, process capabilities?

<--- Score

62. How do controls support value?

<--- Score

63. Implementation Planning: is a pilot needed to test the changes before a full roll out occurs?

<--- Score

64. Is there a infrastructure decisions Communication plan covering who needs to get what information when?

<--- Score

65. Does the infrastructure decisions performance meet the customer's requirements?

<--- Score

66. Who is the infrastructure decisions process owner?

<--- Score

67. Will your goals reflect your program budget?
<--- Score

68. Is knowledge gained on process shared and institutionalized?
<--- Score

69. Will existing staff require re-training, for example, to learn new business processes?
<--- Score

70. How can you best use all of your knowledge repositories to enhance learning and sharing?
<--- Score

71. What are customers monitoring?
<--- Score

72. How will new or emerging customer needs/ requirements be checked/communicated to orient the process toward meeting the new specifications and continually reducing variation?
<--- Score

73. Do you monitor the effectiveness of your infrastructure decisions activities?
<--- Score

74. Is there a transfer of ownership and knowledge to process owner and process team tasked with the responsibilities.
<--- Score

75. What is your plan to assess your security risks?
<--- Score

76. What is the best design framework for infrastructure decisions organization now that, in a post industrial-age if the top-down, command and control model is no longer relevant?
<--- Score

77. Is there documentation that will support the successful operation of the improvement?
<--- Score

78. What should the next improvement project be that is related to infrastructure decisions?
<--- Score

79. Are documented procedures clear and easy to follow for the operators?
<--- Score

80. How do you select, collect, align, and integrate infrastructure decisions data and information for tracking daily operations and overall organizational performance, including progress relative to strategic objectives and action plans?
<--- Score

81. How do you plan on providing proper recognition and disclosure of supporting companies?
<--- Score

82. What are the performance and scale of the infrastructure decisions tools?
<--- Score

83. How will infrastructure decisions decisions be made and monitored?

<--- Score

84. What is the standard for acceptable infrastructure decisions performance?
<--- Score

85. How do you encourage people to take control and responsibility?
<--- Score

86. What should you measure to verify efficiency gains?
<--- Score

87. Who will be in control?
<--- Score

88. How will you measure your QA plan's effectiveness?
<--- Score

89. Is new knowledge gained imbedded in the response plan?
<--- Score

90. How do you spread information?
<--- Score

91. What quality tools were useful in the control phase?
<--- Score

92. Has the improved process and its steps been standardized?
<--- Score

93. In the case of a infrastructure decisions project, the criteria for the audit derive from implementation objectives, an audit of a infrastructure decisions project involves assessing whether the recommendations outlined for implementation have been met, can you track that any infrastructure decisions project is implemented as planned, and is it working?
<--- Score

94. Are new process steps, standards, and documentation ingrained into normal operations?
<--- Score

95. What infrastructure decisions standards are applicable?
<--- Score

96. Do the viable solutions scale to future needs?
<--- Score

97. Who is going to spread your message?
<--- Score

98. How is infrastructure decisions project cost planned, managed, monitored?
<--- Score

Add up total points for this section:
_____ = Total points for this section

Divided by: _____ (number of statements answered) = _____
Average score for this section

Transfer your score to the infrastructure

decisions Index at the beginning of the
Self-Assessment.

CRITERION #7: SUSTAIN:

INTENT: Retain the benefits.

In my belief, the answer to this question is clearly defined:

5 Strongly Agree

4 Agree

3 Neutral

2 Disagree

1 Strongly Disagree

1. How do you go about securing infrastructure decisions?
<--- Score

2. Who uses your product in ways you never expected?
<--- Score

3. Is there any reason to believe the opposite of my current belief?
<--- Score

4. Why should people listen to you?
<--- Score

5. Operational - will it work?
<--- Score

6. Is there any existing infrastructure decisions governance structure?
<--- Score

7. What are the top 3 things at the forefront of your infrastructure decisions agendas for the next 3 years?
<--- Score

8. What potential megatrends could make your business model obsolete?
<--- Score

9. What knowledge, skills and characteristics mark a good infrastructure decisions project manager?
<--- Score

10. Do you think you know, or do you know you know ?
<--- Score

11. Do you think infrastructure decisions accomplishes the goals you expect it to accomplish?
<--- Score

12. If you got fired and a new hire took your place, what would she do different?
<--- Score

13. If you had to rebuild your organization without

any traditional competitive advantages (i.e., no killer technology, promising research, innovative product/ service delivery model, etcetera), how would your people have to approach their work and collaborate together in order to create the necessary conditions for success?

<--- Score

14. What are strategies for increasing support and reducing opposition?

<--- Score

15. Instead of going to current contacts for new ideas, what if you reconnected with dormant contacts-- the people you used to know? If you were going reactivate a dormant tie, who would it be?

<--- Score

16. What new services of functionality will be implemented next with infrastructure decisions ?

<--- Score

17. What are internal and external infrastructure decisions relations?

<--- Score

18. Think of your infrastructure decisions project, what are the main functions?

<--- Score

19. Who will provide the final approval of infrastructure decisions deliverables?

<--- Score

20. In a project to restructure infrastructure decisions outcomes, which stakeholders would

you involve?
<--- Score

21. Is the infrastructure decisions organization completing tasks effectively and efficiently?
<--- Score

22. Who will be responsible for deciding whether infrastructure decisions goes ahead or not after the initial investigations?
<--- Score

23. Are the assumptions believable and achievable?
<--- Score

24. How do you track customer value, profitability or financial return, organizational success, and sustainability?
<--- Score

25. Do you have enough freaky customers in your portfolio pushing you to the limit day in and day out?
<--- Score

26. What is the estimated value of the project?
<--- Score

27. What is your BATNA (best alternative to a negotiated agreement)?
<--- Score

28. What are the long-term infrastructure decisions goals?
<--- Score

29. What is your formula for success in infrastructure

decisions ?

<--- Score

30. Which infrastructure decisions goals are the most important?

<--- Score

31. What are the rules and assumptions your industry operates under? What if the opposite were true?

<--- Score

32. Who is responsible for errors?

<--- Score

33. What are the success criteria that will indicate that infrastructure decisions objectives have been met and the benefits delivered?

<--- Score

34. Is maximizing infrastructure decisions protection the same as minimizing infrastructure decisions loss?

<--- Score

35. Why is it important to have senior management support for a infrastructure decisions project?

<--- Score

36. In the past year, what have you done (or could you have done) to increase the accurate perception of your company/brand as ethical and honest?

<--- Score

37. What trophy do you want on your mantle?

<--- Score

38. Do you see more potential in people than they do in themselves?
<--- Score

39. What are the potential basics of infrastructure decisions fraud?
<--- Score

40. What infrastructure decisions modifications can you make work for you?
<--- Score

41. What you are going to do to affect the numbers?
<--- Score

42. Can you do all this work?
<--- Score

43. How do you lead with infrastructure decisions in mind?
<--- Score

44. What stupid rule would you most like to kill?
<--- Score

45. What relationships among infrastructure decisions trends do you perceive?
<--- Score

46. Are there any activities that you can take off your to do list?
<--- Score

47. How much does infrastructure decisions help?
<--- Score

48. Who do you think the world wants your organization to be?
<--- Score

49. How do you make it meaningful in connecting infrastructure decisions with what users do day-to-day?
<--- Score

50. Who is on the team?
<--- Score

51. What must you excel at?
<--- Score

52. Who, on the executive team or the board, has spoken to a customer recently?
<--- Score

53. What are your personal philosophies regarding infrastructure decisions and how do they influence your work?
<--- Score

54. How will you insure seamless interoperability of infrastructure decisions moving forward?
<--- Score

55. When information truly is ubiquitous, when reach and connectivity are completely global, when computing resources are infinite, and when a whole new set of impossibilities are not only possible, but happening, what will that do to your business?
<--- Score

56. Is it economical; do you have the time and money?
<--- Score

57. What are you challenging?
<--- Score

58. Will it be accepted by users?
<--- Score

59. Do you have an implicit bias for capital investments over people investments?
<--- Score

60. Do infrastructure decisions rules make a reasonable demand on a users capabilities?
<--- Score

61. What does your signature ensure?
<--- Score

62. What information is critical to your organization that your executives are ignoring?
<--- Score

63. How do you stay inspired?
<--- Score

64. How do you keep the momentum going?
<--- Score

65. How will you know that the infrastructure decisions project has been successful?
<--- Score

66. How can you become the company that would put you out of business?

<--- Score

67. Do you have the right capabilities and capacities?
<--- Score

68. What happens at your organization when people fail?
<--- Score

69. What was the last experiment you ran?
<--- Score

70. What is your question? Why?
<--- Score

71. How will you motivate the stakeholders with the least vested interest?
<--- Score

72. How do you determine the key elements that affect infrastructure decisions workforce satisfaction, how are these elements determined for different workforce groups and segments?
<--- Score

73. What is effective infrastructure decisions?
<--- Score

74. How do you provide a safe environment -physically and emotionally?
<--- Score

75. If you weren't already in this business, would you enter it today? And if not, what are you going to do about it?
<--- Score

76. What are the short and long-term infrastructure decisions goals?

<--- Score

77. Are you paying enough attention to the partners your company depends on to succeed?

<--- Score

78. What is the kind of project structure that would be appropriate for your infrastructure decisions project, should it be formal and complex, or can it be less formal and relatively simple?

<--- Score

79. Who do we want your customers to become?

<--- Score

80. What would have to be true for the option on the table to be the best possible choice?

<--- Score

81. Who is responsible for ensuring appropriate resources (time, people and money) are allocated to infrastructure decisions?

<--- Score

82. What could happen if you do not do it?

<--- Score

83. What counts that you are not counting?

<--- Score

84. Is infrastructure decisions realistic, or are you setting yourself up for failure?

<--- Score

85. What are the challenges?
<--- Score

86. If your customer were your grandmother, would you tell her to buy what you're selling?
<--- Score

87. What projects are going on in the organization today, and what resources are those projects using from the resource pools?
<--- Score

88. How do you foster innovation?
<--- Score

89. What is a feasible sequencing of reform initiatives over time?
<--- Score

90. Do you have the right people on the bus?
<--- Score

91. How do you listen to customers to obtain actionable information?
<--- Score

92. What happens when a new employee joins the organization?
<--- Score

93. Are the criteria for selecting recommendations stated?
<--- Score

94. How do you foster the skills, knowledge, talents,

attributes, and characteristics you want to have?
<--- Score

95. How do you create buy-in?
<--- Score

96. Whom among your colleagues do you trust, and for what?
<--- Score

97. What are current infrastructure decisions paradigms?
<--- Score

98. Who is the main stakeholder, with ultimate responsibility for driving infrastructure decisions forward?
<--- Score

99. What trouble can you get into?
<--- Score

100. What unique value proposition (UVP) do you offer?
<--- Score

101. Did your employees make progress today?
<--- Score

102. What are specific infrastructure decisions rules to follow?
<--- Score

103. How do you maintain infrastructure decisions's Integrity?
<--- Score

104. What is the range of capabilities?
<--- Score

105. What is it like to work for you?
<--- Score

106. How do customers see your organization?
<--- Score

107. Who else should you help?
<--- Score

108. How do you set infrastructure decisions stretch targets and how do you get people to not only participate in setting these stretch targets but also that they strive to achieve these?
<--- Score

109. What are the gaps in your knowledge and experience?
<--- Score

110. What is your competitive advantage?
<--- Score

111. Where can you break convention?
<--- Score

112. Which functions and people interact with the supplier and or customer?
<--- Score

113. Do you say no to customers for no reason?
<--- Score

114. What is the overall business strategy?
<--- Score

115. How do you deal with infrastructure decisions changes?
<--- Score

116. How is implementation research currently incorporated into each of your goals?
<--- Score

117. What are the essentials of internal infrastructure decisions management?
<--- Score

118. If your company went out of business tomorrow, would anyone who doesn't get a paycheck here care?
<--- Score

119. What is the recommended frequency of auditing?
<--- Score

120. Ask yourself: how would you do this work if you only had one staff member to do it?
<--- Score

121. If you had to leave your organization for a year and the only communication you could have with employees/colleagues was a single paragraph, what would you write?
<--- Score

122. Which individuals, teams or departments will be involved in infrastructure decisions?
<--- Score

123. How will you ensure you get what you expected?
<--- Score

124. Can the schedule be done in the given time?
<--- Score

125. What role does communication play in the success or failure of a infrastructure decisions project?
<--- Score

126. If you find that you havent accomplished one of the goals for one of the steps of the infrastructure decisions strategy, what will you do to fix it?
<--- Score

127. How do you accomplish your long range infrastructure decisions goals?
<--- Score

128. What are the business goals infrastructure decisions is aiming to achieve?
<--- Score

129. What is the craziest thing you can do?
<--- Score

130. How can you incorporate support to ensure safe and effective use of infrastructure decisions into the services that you provide?
<--- Score

131. What threat is infrastructure decisions addressing?
<--- Score

132. What one word do you want to own in the minds of your customers, employees, and partners?
<--- Score

133. How do you engage the workforce, in addition to satisfying them?
<--- Score

134. If you were responsible for initiating and implementing major changes in your organization, what steps might you take to ensure acceptance of those changes?
<--- Score

135. If you do not follow, then how to lead?
<--- Score

136. What are the key enablers to make this infrastructure decisions move?
<--- Score

137. Why is infrastructure decisions important for you now?
<--- Score

138. How do you govern and fulfill your societal responsibilities?
<--- Score

139. Are all key stakeholders present at all Structured Walkthroughs?
<--- Score

140. Are you maintaining a past–present–future perspective throughout the infrastructure decisions discussion?

<--- Score

141. Who are the key stakeholders?
<--- Score

142. At what moment would you think; Will I get fired?
<--- Score

143. How are you doing compared to your industry?
<--- Score

144. Which models, tools and techniques are necessary?
<--- Score

145. Who have you, as a company, historically been when you've been at your best?
<--- Score

146. What is the purpose of infrastructure decisions in relation to the mission?
<--- Score

147. Is a infrastructure decisions team work effort in place?
<--- Score

148. Political -is anyone trying to undermine this project?
<--- Score

149. Do you have past infrastructure decisions successes?
<--- Score

150. What will be the consequences to the

stakeholder (financial, reputation etc) if infrastructure decisions does not go ahead or fails to deliver the objectives?
<--- Score

151. How long will it take to change?
<--- Score

152. Is your basic point _____ or _____?
<--- Score

153. Has implementation been effective in reaching specified objectives so far?
<--- Score

154. What are your most important goals for the strategic infrastructure decisions objectives?
<--- Score

155. What are the barriers to increased infrastructure decisions production?
<--- Score

156. Are you making progress, and are you making progress as infrastructure decisions leaders?
<--- Score

157. What should you stop doing?
<--- Score

158. What management system can you use to leverage the infrastructure decisions experience, ideas, and concerns of the people closest to the work to be done?
<--- Score

159. How do you proactively clarify deliverables and infrastructure decisions quality expectations?
<--- Score

160. What happens if you do not have enough funding?
<--- Score

161. How can you become more high-tech but still be high touch?
<--- Score

162. How do you transition from the baseline to the target?
<--- Score

163. Is there a work around that you can use?
<--- Score

164. To whom do you add value?
<--- Score

165. What have you done to protect your business from competitive encroachment?
<--- Score

166. How do senior leaders deploy your organizations vision and values through your leadership system, to the workforce, to key suppliers and partners, and to customers and other stakeholders, as appropriate?
<--- Score

167. If there were zero limitations, what would you do differently?
<--- Score

168. Who will determine interim and final deadlines?
<--- Score

169. Why not do infrastructure decisions?
<--- Score

170. Who will manage the integration of tools?
<--- Score

171. What is something you believe that nearly no one agrees with you on?
<--- Score

172. What is the overall talent health of your organization as a whole at senior levels, and for each organization reporting to a member of the Senior Leadership Team?
<--- Score

173. What goals did you miss?
<--- Score

174. Is infrastructure decisions dependent on the successful delivery of a current project?
<--- Score

175. Why do and why don't your customers like your organization?
<--- Score

176. Is your strategy driving your strategy? Or is the way in which you allocate resources driving your strategy?
<--- Score

177. Who are your customers?

<--- Score

178. Are you / should you be revolutionary or evolutionary?
<--- Score

179. How likely is it that a customer would recommend your company to a friend or colleague?
<--- Score

180. How do you keep records, of what?
<--- Score

181. What are you trying to prove to yourself, and how might it be hijacking your life and business success?
<--- Score

182. Can you maintain your growth without detracting from the factors that have contributed to your success?
<--- Score

183. Who are four people whose careers you have enhanced?
<--- Score

184. How do you ensure that implementations of infrastructure decisions products are done in a way that ensures safety?
<--- Score

185. Are assumptions made in infrastructure decisions stated explicitly?
<--- Score

186. Would you rather sell to knowledgeable and informed customers or to uninformed customers?
<--- Score

187. What infrastructure decisions skills are most important?
<--- Score

188. How can you negotiate infrastructure decisions successfully with a stubborn boss, an irate client, or a deceitful coworker?
<--- Score

189. Do you feel that more should be done in the infrastructure decisions area?
<--- Score

190. Who do you want your customers to become?
<--- Score

191. How much contingency will be available in the budget?
<--- Score

192. What business benefits will infrastructure decisions goals deliver if achieved?
<--- Score

193. Whose voice (department, ethnic group, women, older workers, etc) might you have missed hearing from in your company, and how might you amplify this voice to create positive momentum for your business?
<--- Score

194. What is an unauthorized commitment?

<--- Score

Add up total points for this section:
_____ = Total points for this section

Divided by: _____ (number of
statements answered) = _____
Average score for this section

Transfer your score to the infrastructure
decisions Index at the beginning of the
Self-Assessment.

Infrastructure Decisions and Managing Projects, Criteria for Project Managers:

1.0 Initiating Process Group: Infrastructure Decisions

1. Do you know all the stakeholders impacted by the Infrastructure Decisions project and what needs are?

2. Specific - is the objective clear in terms of what, how, when, and where the situation will be changed?

3. The process to Manage Stakeholders is part of which process group?

4. What will you do to minimize the impact should a risk event occur?

5. Were resources available as planned?

6. How well did you do?

7. During which stage of Risk planning are risks prioritized based on probability and impact?

8. What were things that you did well, and could improve, and how?

9. What are the pressing issues of the hour?

10. What were things that you did very well and want to do the same again on the next Infrastructure Decisions project?

11. Did the Infrastructure Decisions project team have the right skills?

12. When must it be done?

13. How do you help others satisfy needs?

14. In which Infrastructure Decisions project management process group is the detailed Infrastructure Decisions project budget created?

15. Are the changes in your Infrastructure Decisions project being formally requested, analyzed, and approved by the appropriate decision makers?

16. At which cmmi level are software processes documented, standardized, and integrated into a standard to-be practiced process for your organization?

17. Do you know the Infrastructure Decisions projects goal, purpose and objectives?

18. Who are the Infrastructure Decisions project stakeholders?

19. What areas were overlooked on this Infrastructure Decisions project?

20. Are you certain deliverables are properly completed and meet quality standards?

1.1 Project Charter: Infrastructure Decisions

21. Run it as as a startup?

22. Name and describe the elements that deal with providing the detail?

23. When will this occur?

24. What does it need to do?

25. What is the purpose of the Infrastructure Decisions project?

26. How will you know that a change is an improvement?

27. Who is the sponsor?

28. What changes can you make to improve?

29. Who will take notes, document decisions?

30. What is the justification?

31. What are you striving to accomplish (measurable goal(s))?

32. What are the constraints?

33. Where and how does the team fit within your organization structure?

34. Is it an improvement over existing products?

35. If finished, on what date did it finish?

36. Why do you need to manage scope?

37. Infrastructure Decisions project background: what is the primary motivation for this Infrastructure Decisions project?

38. Why have you chosen the aim you have set forth?

39. Who is the Infrastructure Decisions project Manager?

40. Customer benefits: what customer requirements does this Infrastructure Decisions project address?

1.2 Stakeholder Register: Infrastructure Decisions

41. Is your organization ready for change?

42. What & Why?

43. Who wants to talk about Security?

44. How should employers make voices heard?

45. What opportunities exist to provide communications?

46. What are the major Infrastructure Decisions project milestones requiring communications or providing communications opportunities?

47. How big is the gap?

48. What is the power of the stakeholder?

49. Who are the stakeholders?

50. Who is managing stakeholder engagement?

51. How will reports be created?

52. How much influence do they have on the Infrastructure Decisions project?

1.3 Stakeholder Analysis Matrix: Infrastructure Decisions

53. How are you predicting what future (work)loads will be?

54. What is the relationship among stakeholders?

55. Are the interests in line with the program objectives?

56. Competitors vulnerabilities?

57. Does the stakeholder want to be involved or merely need to be informed about the Infrastructure Decisions project and its process?

58. What is the range you need to look at?

59. Insurmountable weaknesses?

60. What is your Risk Management?

61. How do you manage Infrastructure Decisions project Risk?

62. Market demand?

63. Who will be affected by the Infrastructure Decisions project?

64. What are the reimbursement requirements?

65. Niche target markets?

66. Market developments?

67. How much do resources cost?

68. Do any safeguard policies apply to the Infrastructure Decisions project?

69. Participatory approach: how will key stakeholders participate in the Infrastructure Decisions project?

70. Is there a clear description of the scope of practice of the Infrastructure Decisions projects educators?

71. Are the required specifications for products or services changing?

72. What do people from other organizations see as your organizations weaknesses?

2.0 Planning Process Group: Infrastructure Decisions

73. To what extent is the program helping to influence your organizations policy framework?

74. What are the different approaches to building the WBS?

75. To what extent are the visions and actions of the partners consistent or divergent with regard to the program?

76. Is the pace of implementing the products of the program ensuring the completeness of the results of the Infrastructure Decisions project?

77. What factors are contributing to progress or delay in the achievement of products and results?

78. Did you read it correctly?

79. How will you know you did it?

80. Why is it important to determine activity sequencing on Infrastructure Decisions projects?

81. Does it make any difference if you are successful?

82. What makes your Infrastructure Decisions project successful?

83. Who are the Infrastructure Decisions project

stakeholders?

84. What should you do next?

85. Does the program have follow-up mechanisms (to verify the quality of the products, punctuality of delivery, etc.) to measure progress in the achievement of the envisaged results?

86. What is a Software Development Life Cycle (SDLC)?

87. In what way has the Infrastructure Decisions project come up with innovative measures for problem-solving?

88. What is the difference between the early schedule and late schedule?

89. In which Infrastructure Decisions project management process group is the detailed Infrastructure Decisions project budget created?

90. What input will you be required to provide the Infrastructure Decisions project team?

91. What do they need to know about the Infrastructure Decisions project?

2.1 Project Management Plan: Infrastructure Decisions

92. What would you do differently?

93. Does the implementation plan have an appropriate division of responsibilities?

94. If the Infrastructure Decisions project is complex or scope is specialized, do you have appropriate and/or qualified staff available to perform the tasks?

95. Are there non-structural buyout or relocation recommendations?

96. Are comparable cost estimates used for comparing, screening and selecting alternative plans, and has a reasonable cost estimate been developed for the recommended plan?

97. Do there need to be organizational changes?

98. Why Change?

99. What is the business need?

100. What worked well?

101. Does the selected plan protect privacy?

102. How do you manage time?

103. When is the Infrastructure Decisions project

management plan created?

104. What if, for example, the positive direction and vision of your organization causes expected trends to change resulting in greater need than expected?

105. What are the assigned resources?

106. How do you manage integration?

107. Is there anything you would now do differently on your Infrastructure Decisions project based on past experience?

108. Is there an incremental analysis/cost effectiveness analysis of proposed mitigation features based on an approved method and using an accepted model?

109. Are there any windfall benefits that would accrue to the Infrastructure Decisions project sponsor or other parties?

110. What went wrong?

2.2 Scope Management Plan: Infrastructure Decisions

111. Are vendor contract reports, reviews and visits conducted periodically?

112. Does the Infrastructure Decisions project have a Statement of Work?

113. Are adequate resources provided for the quality assurance function?

114. Are the budget estimates reasonable?

115. Are actuals compared against estimates to analyze and correct variances?

116. Are issues raised, assessed, actioned, and resolved in a timely and efficient manner?

117. Has a Infrastructure Decisions project Communications Plan been developed?

118. Did your Infrastructure Decisions project ask for this?

119. Staffing Requirements?

120. Are tasks tracked by hours?

121. Alignment to strategic goals & objectives?

122. Do you secure formal approval of changes and

requirements from stakeholders?

123. Have all documents been archived in a Infrastructure Decisions project repository for each release?

124. How relevant is this attribute to this Infrastructure Decisions project or audit?

125. Is there any form of automated support for Issues Management?

126. How will scope changes be identified and classified?

127. Where do scope management processes fit in?

128. Are post milestone Infrastructure Decisions project reviews (PMPR) conducted with your organization at least once a year?

129. Are estimating assumptions and constraints captured?

130. Are milestone deliverables effectively tracked and compared to Infrastructure Decisions project plan?

2.3 Requirements Management Plan: Infrastructure Decisions

131. What performance metrics will be used?

132. Why manage requirements?

133. Have stakeholders been instructed in the Change Control process?

134. How will unresolved questions be handled once approval has been obtained?

135. Did you use declarative statements?

136. Who will do the reporting and to whom will reports be delivered?

137. Who will perform the analysis?

138. Is requirements work dependent on any other specific Infrastructure Decisions project or non-Infrastructure Decisions project activities (e.g. funding, approvals, procurement)?

139. Describe the process for rejecting the Infrastructure Decisions project requirements. Who has the authority to reject Infrastructure Decisions project requirements?

140. Will the Infrastructure Decisions project requirements become approved in writing?

141. Business analysis scope?

142. How knowledgeable is the team in the proposed application area?

143. Are actual resource expenditures versus planned still acceptable?

144. Will you use tracing to help understand the impact of a change in requirements?

145. The wbs is developed as part of a joint planning session. and how do you know that youhave done this right?

146. Will you document changes to requirements?

147. Do you expect stakeholders to be cooperative?

148. Controlling Infrastructure Decisions project requirements involves monitoring the status of the Infrastructure Decisions project requirements and managing changes to the requirements. Who is responsible for monitoring and tracking the Infrastructure Decisions project requirements?

149. How will the requirements become prioritized?

2.4 Requirements Documentation: Infrastructure Decisions

150. Does the system provide the functions which best support the customers needs?

151. Has requirements gathering uncovered information that would necessitate changes?

152. The problem with gathering requirements is right there in the word gathering. What images does it conjure?

153. Can the requirement be changed without a large impact on other requirements?

154. Basic work/business process; high-level, what is being touched?

155. What is the risk associated with cost and schedule?

156. Verifiability. can the requirements be checked?

157. How will the proposed Infrastructure Decisions project help?

158. How do you get the user to tell you what they want?

159. Can you check system requirements?

160. Who is involved?

161. What variations exist for a process?

162. What can tools do for us?

163. What marketing channels do you want to use: e-mail, letter or sms?

164. Where do system and software requirements come from, what are sources?

165. Can the requirements be checked?

166. What images does it conjure?

167. Completeness. are all functions required by the customer included?

168. How will they be documented / shared?

169. How much does requirements engineering cost?

2.5 Requirements Traceability Matrix: Infrastructure Decisions

170. Do you have a clear understanding of all subcontracts in place?

171. Is there a requirements traceability process in place?

172. What is the WBS?

173. What percentage of Infrastructure Decisions projects are producing traceability matrices between requirements and other work products?

174. How do you manage scope?

175. Describe the process for approving requirements so they can be added to the traceability matrix and Infrastructure Decisions project work can be performed. Will the Infrastructure Decisions project requirements become approved in writing?

176. Will you use a Requirements Traceability Matrix?

177. How will it affect the stakeholders personally in career?

178. How small is small enough?

179. What are the chronologies, contingencies, consequences, criteria?

180. Why do you manage scope?

181. Why use a WBS?

2.6 Project Scope Statement: Infrastructure Decisions

182. Is an issue management process documented and filed?

183. How often will scope changes be reviewed?

184. Is the quality function identified and assigned?

185. Is there an information system for the Infrastructure Decisions project?

186. Elements of scope management that deal with concept development ?

187. Who will you recommend approve the change, and when do you recommend the change reviews occur?

188. If you were to write a list of what should not be included in the scope statement, what are the things that you would recommend be described as out-of-scope?

189. Did your Infrastructure Decisions project ask for this?

190. Are there backup strategies for key members of the Infrastructure Decisions project?

191. Are there specific processes you will use to evaluate and approve/reject changes?

192. What process would you recommend for creating the Infrastructure Decisions project scope statement?

193. Change management vs. change leadership - what is the difference?

194. Is there a Change Management Board?

195. Will there be a Change Control Process in place?

196. What are the possible consequences should a risk come to occur?

197. What went right?

198. Will the risk status be reported to management on a regular and frequent basis?

199. Risks?

200. Will the risk plan be updated on a regular and frequent basis?

2.7 Assumption and Constraint Log: Infrastructure Decisions

201. Violation trace: why ?

202. What strengths do you have?

203. Were the system requirements formally reviewed prior to initiating the design phase?

204. Is there documentation of system capability requirements, data requirements, environment requirements, security requirements, and computer and hardware requirements?

205. What is positive about the current process?

206. What if failure during recovery?

207. Has a Infrastructure Decisions project Communications Plan been developed?

208. What do you audit?

209. Have you eliminated all duplicative tasks or manual efforts, where appropriate?

210. Does the document/deliverable meet all requirements (for example, statement of work) specific to this deliverable?

211. Can you perform this task or activity in a more effective manner?

212. Would known impacts serve as impediments?

213. Are there processes defining how software will be developed including development methods, overall timeline for development, software product standards, and traceability?

214. Is this model reasonable?

215. What do you log?

216. Have all stakeholders been identified?

217. Are there processes in place to ensure that all the terms and code concepts have been documented consistently?

218. Is this process still needed?

219. Is there adequate stakeholder participation for the vetting of requirements definition, changes and management?

2.8 Work Breakdown Structure: Infrastructure Decisions

220. Why would you develop a Work Breakdown Structure?

221. Is it a change in scope?

222. How much detail?

223. Where does it take place?

224. How big is a work-package?

225. Who has to do it?

226. What is the probability that the Infrastructure Decisions project duration will exceed xx weeks?

227. How many levels?

228. When do you stop?

229. When does it have to be done?

230. Why is it useful?

231. How far down?

232. What is the probability of completing the Infrastructure Decisions project in less that xx days?

233. What has to be done?

234. When would you develop a Work Breakdown
Structure?

2.9 WBS Dictionary: Infrastructure Decisions

235. Are procedures established to prevent changes to the contract budget base other than the already stated authorized by contractual action?

236. Knowledgeable Infrastructure Decisions projections of future performance?

237. Are time-phased budgets established for planning and control of level of effort activity by category of resource; for example, type of manpower and/or material?

238. Is budgeted cost for work performed calculated in a manner consistent with the way work is planned?

239. Are overhead cost budgets (or Infrastructure Decisions projections) established on a facility-wide basis at least annually for the life of the contract?

240. Does the contractors system provide for accurate cost accumulation and assignment to control accounts in a manner consistent with the budgets using recognized acceptable costing techniques?

241. Are internal budgets for authorized, and not priced changes based on the contractors resource plan for accomplishing the work?

242. Changes in the overhead pool and/or organization structures?

243. Is cost performance measurement at the point in time most suitable for the category of material involved, and no earlier than the time of actual receipt of material?

244. Identify potential or actual budget-based and time-based schedule variances?

245. Are work packages reasonably short in time duration or do they have adequate objective indicators/milestones to minimize subjectivity of the in process work evaluation?

246. Does the contractors system description or procedures require that the performance measurement baseline plus management reserve equal the contract budget base?

247. Identify and isolate causes of favorable and unfavorable cost and schedule variances?

248. Time-phased control account budgets?

249. Should you have a test for each code module?

250. Appropriate work authorization documents which subdivide the contractual effort and responsibilities, within functional organizations?

251. Budgeted cost for work performed?

252. The anticipated business volume?

253. What is wrong with this Infrastructure Decisions project?

2.10 Schedule Management Plan: Infrastructure Decisions

254. Has the Infrastructure Decisions project scope been baselined?

255. Are target dates established for each milestone deliverable?

256. Have stakeholder accountabilities & responsibilities been clearly defined?

257. Are metrics used to evaluate and manage Vendors?

258. Has process improvement efforts been completed before requirements efforts begin?

259. Are all attributes of the activities defined, including risk and uncertainty?

260. Does the Infrastructure Decisions project have a Statement of Work?

261. Has a quality assurance plan been developed for the Infrastructure Decisions project?

262. Has your organization readiness assessment been conducted?

263. Is there a requirements change management processes in place?

264. Are non-critical path items updated and agreed upon with the teams?

265. Define units of measurement for each resource. For example, are you referencing gallons or liters?

266. Does the detailed work plan match the complexity of tasks with the capabilities of personnel?

267. Are written status reports provided on a designated frequent basis?

268. Are the key elements of a Infrastructure Decisions project Charter present?

269. Has the Infrastructure Decisions project manager been identified?

270. Are cause and effect determined for risks when they occur?

271. Is there an excessive and invalid use of task constraints and relationships of leads/lags?

272. Has the ims been resource-loaded and are assigned resources reasonable and available?

273. Are scheduled deliverables actually delivered?

2.11 Activity List: Infrastructure Decisions

274. How detailed should a Infrastructure Decisions project get?

275. What is your organizations history in doing similar activities?

276. Is infrastructure setup part of your Infrastructure Decisions project?

277. How can the Infrastructure Decisions project be displayed graphically to better visualize the activities?

278. What is the LF and LS for each activity?

279. When do the individual activities need to start and finish?

280. When will the work be performed?

281. What is the total time required to complete the Infrastructure Decisions project if no delays occur?

282. What is the probability the Infrastructure Decisions project can be completed in xx weeks?

283. What did not go as well?

284. In what sequence?

285. Who will perform the work?

286. What are you counting on?

287. What will be performed?

288. Are the required resources available or need to be acquired?

289. How will it be performed?

290. How difficult will it be to do specific activities on this Infrastructure Decisions project?

2.12 Activity Attributes: Infrastructure Decisions

291. Activity: fair or not fair?

292. Does your organization of the data change its meaning?

293. Is there a trend during the year?

294. How much activity detail is required?

295. Is there anything planned that does not need to be here?

296. Activity: what is In the Bag?

297. How many days do you need to complete the work scope with a limit of X number of resources?

298. Are the required resources available?

299. Has management defined a definite timeframe for the turnaround or Infrastructure Decisions project window?

300. What is missing?

301. Would you consider either of corresponding activities an outlier?

302. Where else does it apply?

303. How difficult will it be to do specific activities on this Infrastructure Decisions project?

304. Activity: what is Missing?

305. Which method produces the more accurate cost assignment?

306. How many resources do you need to complete the work scope within a limit of X number of days?

307. What activity do you think you should spend the most time on?

2.13 Milestone List: Infrastructure Decisions

308. Legislative effects?

309. What background experience, skills, and strengths does the team bring to your organization?

310. Who will manage the Infrastructure Decisions project on a day-to-day basis?

311. What has been done so far?

312. Gaps in capabilities?

313. Calculate how long can activity be delayed?

314. Obstacles faced?

315. How difficult will it be to do specific activities on this Infrastructure Decisions project?

316. Do you foresee any technical risks or developmental challenges?

317. What are your competitors vulnerabilities?

318. Which path is the critical path?

319. How will you get the word out to customers?

320. Describe your organizations strengths and core competencies. What factors will make your

organization succeed?

321. Competitive advantages?

322. How soon can the activity start?

323. Timescales, deadlines and pressures?

324. What would happen if a delivery of material was one week late?

325. Level of the Innovation?

2.14 Network Diagram: Infrastructure Decisions

326. What is the completion time?

327. What job or jobs precede it?

328. What is the lowest cost to complete this Infrastructure Decisions project in xx weeks?

329. Planning: who, how long, what to do?

330. How confident can you be in your milestone dates and the delivery date?

331. Are you on time?

332. If the Infrastructure Decisions project network diagram cannot change and you have extra personnel resources, what is the BEST thing to do?

333. Exercise: what is the probability that the Infrastructure Decisions project duration will exceed xx weeks?

334. What activities must occur simultaneously with this activity?

335. Can you calculate the confidence level?

336. What activity must be completed immediately before this activity can start?

337. Why must you schedule milestones, such as reviews, throughout the Infrastructure Decisions project?

338. What activities must follow this activity?

339. Are the gantt chart and/or network diagram updated periodically and used to assess the overall Infrastructure Decisions project timetable?

340. What are the Key Success Factors?

341. Where do schedules come from?

342. What must be completed before an activity can be started?

343. What to do and When?

344. What controls the start and finish of a job?

2.15 Activity Resource Requirements: Infrastructure Decisions

345. Which logical relationship does the PDM use most often?

346. Are there unresolved issues that need to be addressed?

347. Time for overtime?

348. Do you use tools like decomposition and rolling-wave planning to produce the activity list and other outputs?

349. When does monitoring begin?

350. Other support in specific areas?

351. Organizational Applicability?

352. How do you handle petty cash?

353. Why do you do that?

354. How many signatures do you require on a check and does this match what is in your policy and procedures?

355. What is the Work Plan Standard?

356. Anything else?

357. What are constraints that you might find during the Human Resource Planning process?

2.16 Resource Breakdown Structure: Infrastructure Decisions

358. How can this help you with team building?

359. When do they need the information?

360. What can you do to improve productivity?

361. Is predictive resource analysis being done?

362. How difficult will it be to do specific activities on this Infrastructure Decisions project?

363. Who delivers the information?

364. Why do you do it?

365. What is the difference between % Complete and % work?

366. What is each stakeholders desired outcome for the Infrastructure Decisions project?

367. What defines a successful Infrastructure Decisions project?

368. Which resource planning tool provides information on resource responsibility and accountability?

369. What defines a successful Infrastructure Decisions project?

370. Who needs what information?

371. Who is allowed to see what data about which resources?

372. What is the primary purpose of the human resource plan?

373. What are the requirements for resource data?

374. Who is allowed to perform which functions?

2.17 Activity Duration Estimates: Infrastructure Decisions

375. What is the duration of a milestone?

376. Which type of mathematical analysis is being used?

377. After changes are approved are Infrastructure Decisions project documents updated and distributed?

378. Which is correct?

379. Which is a benefit of an analogous Infrastructure Decisions project estimate?

380. If you plan to take the PMP exam soon, what should you do to prepare?

381. What do you think about the WBSs for them?

382. What are the nine areas of expertise?

383. What is the BEST thing for the Infrastructure Decisions project manager to do?

384. What are the typical challenges Infrastructure Decisions project teams face during each of the five process groups?

385. Are contractor costs, schedule and technical performance monitored throughout the

Infrastructure Decisions project?

386. See what went wrong?

387. If the optimiztic estimate for an activity is 12days, and the pessimistic estimate is 18days, what is the standard deviation of this activity?

388. Are risks that are likely to affect the Infrastructure Decisions project identified and documented?

389. Why is it important to determine activity sequencing on Infrastructure Decisions projects?

390. What questions do you have about the sample documents provided?

391. Are resource rates available to calculate Infrastructure Decisions project costs?

392. Are procedures defined for calculating cost estimates?

393. Calculate the expected duration for an activity that has a most likely time of 3, a pessimistic time of 10, and a optimiztic time of 2?

2.18 Duration Estimating Worksheet: Infrastructure Decisions

394. Small or large Infrastructure Decisions project?

395. Is the Infrastructure Decisions project responsive to community need?

396. Why estimate time and cost?

397. Does the Infrastructure Decisions project provide innovative ways for stakeholders to overcome obstacles or deliver better outcomes?

398. When does your organization expect to be able to complete it?

399. Will the Infrastructure Decisions project collaborate with the local community and leverage resources?

400. What are the critical bottleneck activities?

401. Why estimate costs?

402. What work will be included in the Infrastructure Decisions project?

403. What utility impacts are there?

404. Value pocket identification & quantification what are value pockets?

405. For other activities, how much delay can be tolerated?

406. What is an Average Infrastructure Decisions project?

407. Define the work as completely as possible. What work will be included in the Infrastructure Decisions project?

408. Science = process: remember the scientific method?

409. How can the Infrastructure Decisions project be displayed graphically to better visualize the activities?

410. What is the total time required to complete the Infrastructure Decisions project if no delays occur?

411. What is next?

412. What questions do you have?

2.19 Project Schedule: Infrastructure Decisions

413. What is Infrastructure Decisions project management?

414. Are procedures defined by which the Infrastructure Decisions project schedule may be changed?

415. Why or why not?

416. How can you minimize or control changes to Infrastructure Decisions project schedules?

417. Did the final product meet or exceed user expectations?

418. Understand the constraints used in preparing the schedule. Are activities connected because logic dictates the order in which others occur?

419. Is there a Schedule Management Plan that establishes the criteria and activities for developing, monitoring and controlling the Infrastructure Decisions project schedule?

420. Are key risk mitigation strategies added to the Infrastructure Decisions project schedule?

421. Why do you think schedule issues often cause the most conflicts on Infrastructure Decisions projects?

422. Should you include sub-activities?

423. If you can not fix it, how do you do it differently?

424. If there are any qualifying green components to this Infrastructure Decisions project, what portion of the total Infrastructure Decisions project cost is green?

425. Why is this particularly bad?

426. Is the Infrastructure Decisions project schedule available for all Infrastructure Decisions project team members to review?

427. Have all Infrastructure Decisions project delays been adequately accounted for, communicated to all stakeholders and adjustments made in overall Infrastructure Decisions project schedule?

428. Are you working on the right risks?

429. What is the most mis-scheduled part of process?

430. Change management required?

431. Meet requirements?

2.20 Cost Management Plan: Infrastructure Decisions

432. Escalation criteria met?

433. Are the Infrastructure Decisions project plans updated on a frequent basis?

434. Responsibilities – what is the split of responsibilities between the owner and contractors?

435. Forecasts – how will the cost to complete the Infrastructure Decisions project be forecast?

436. Is the assigned Infrastructure Decisions project manager a PMP (Certified Infrastructure Decisions project manager) and experienced?

437. Has the budget been baselined?

438. What would the life cycle costs be?

439. Are changes in deliverable commitments agreed to by all affected groups & individuals?

440. Are assumptions being identified, recorded, analyzed, qualified and closed?

441. Are post milestone Infrastructure Decisions project reviews (PMPR) conducted with your organization at least once a year?

442. Are enough systems & user personnel assigned

to the Infrastructure Decisions project?

443. How difficult will it be to do specific tasks on the Infrastructure Decisions project?

444. Infrastructure Decisions project Objectives?

445. Are change requests logged and managed?

446. Are staff skills known and available for each task?

447. Do all stakeholders know how to access this repository and where to find the Infrastructure Decisions project documentation?

448. Are the appropriate IT resources adequate to meet planned commitments?

2.21 Activity Cost Estimates: Infrastructure Decisions

449. How do you fund change orders?

450. Were decisions made in a timely manner?

451. What are the audit requirements?

452. What makes a good expected result statement?

453. What is included in indirect cost being allocated?

454. Will you need to provide essential services information about activities?

455. What happens if you cannot produce the documentation for the single audit?

456. Can you change your activities?

457. Who determines when the contractor is paid?

458. The impact and what actions were taken?

459. Certification of actual expenditures?

460. What cost data should be used to estimate costs during the 2-year follow-up period?

461. Are cost subtotals needed?

462. Based on your Infrastructure Decisions project

communication management plan, what worked well?

463. What do you want to know about the stay to know if costs were inappropriately high or low?

464. Eac -estimate at completion, what is the total job expected to cost?

465. What makes a good activity description?

466. Did the Infrastructure Decisions project team have the right skills?

2.22 Cost Estimating Worksheet: Infrastructure Decisions

467. What is the purpose of estimating?

468. What happens to any remaining funds not used?

469. What is the estimated labor cost today based upon this information?

470. Does the Infrastructure Decisions project provide innovative ways for stakeholders to overcome obstacles or deliver better outcomes?

471. Can a trend be established from historical performance data on the selected measure and are the criteria for using trend analysis or forecasting methods met?

472. What will others want?

473. What additional Infrastructure Decisions project(s) could be initiated as a result of this Infrastructure Decisions project?

474. Is it feasible to establish a control group arrangement?

475. Ask: are others positioned to know, are others credible, and will others cooperate?

476. What costs are to be estimated?

477. Will the Infrastructure Decisions project collaborate with the local community and leverage resources?

478. Who is best positioned to know and assist in identifying corresponding factors?

479. Identify the timeframe necessary to monitor progress and collect data to determine how the selected measure has changed?

480. What can be included?

481. How will the results be shared and to whom?

482. Is the Infrastructure Decisions project responsive to community need?

483. What info is needed?

2.23 Cost Baseline: Infrastructure Decisions

484. Have the resources used by the Infrastructure Decisions project been reassigned to other units or Infrastructure Decisions projects?

485. How fast?

486. Will the Infrastructure Decisions project fail if the change request is not executed?

487. Definition of done can be traced back to the definitions of what are you providing to the customer in terms of deliverables?

488. Verify business objectives. Are others appropriate, and well-articulated?

489. Has the documentation relating to operation and maintenance of the product(s) or service(s) been delivered to, and accepted by, operations management?

490. Should a more thorough impact analysis be conducted?

491. Infrastructure Decisions project goals -should others be reconsidered?

492. What do you want to measure ?

493. Are you meeting with your team regularly?

494. How concrete were original objectives?

495. Who will use corresponding metrics ?

496. At which frequency ?

497. Pcs for your new business. what would the life cycle costs be?

498. Review your risk triggers -have your risks changed?

499. What weaknesses do you have?

500. What is cost and Infrastructure Decisions project cost management?

501. What is it ?

2.24 Quality Management Plan: Infrastructure Decisions

502. How effectively was the Quality Management Plan applied during Infrastructure Decisions project Execution?

503. How long do you retain data?

504. How is the information recorded?

505. List your organizations customer contact standards that employees are expected to maintain. How are corresponding standards measured?

506. Are requirements management tracking tools and procedures in place?

507. Contradictory information between document sections?

508. How do you field-modify testing procedures?

509. How relevant is this attribute to this Infrastructure Decisions project or audit?

510. Who needs a qmp?

511. What is the Quality Management Plan?

512. After observing execution of process, is it in compliance with the documented Plan?

513. What is your organizations strategic planning process?

514. What key performance indicators does your organization use to measure, manage, and improve key processes?

515. Are you meeting your customers expectations consistently?

516. How does your organization measure customer satisfaction/dissatisfaction?

517. Are there trends or hot spots?

518. Who is responsible for approving the qapp?

519. When reporting to different audiences, do you vary the form or type of report?

2.25 Quality Metrics: Infrastructure Decisions

520. How can the effectiveness of each of the activities be measured?

521. What are your organizations next steps?

522. How exactly do you define when differences exist?

523. What can manufacturing professionals do to ensure quality is seen as an integral part of the entire product lifecycle?

524. What is the CMS Benchmark?

525. Do the operators focus on determining; is there anything you need to worry about?

526. How do you calculate corresponding metrics?

527. What is the timeline to meet your goal?

528. Are documents on hand to provide explanations of privacy and confidentiality?

529. What method of measurement do you use?

530. What is the benchmark?

531. Was review conducted per standard protocols?

532. How do you measure?

533. What if the biggest risk to your business were the already stated people who do not complain?

534. Are interface issues coordinated?

535. Can visual measures help you to filter visualizations of interest?

536. Which are the right metrics to use?

537. Are quality metrics defined?

538. Does risk analysis documentation meet standards?

539. What metrics do you measure?

2.26 Process Improvement Plan: Infrastructure Decisions

540. Have storage and access mechanisms and procedures been determined?

541. What is the test-cycle concept?

542. Are you making progress on your improvement plan?

543. If a process improvement framework is being used, which elements will help the problems and goals listed?

544. What personnel are the champions for the initiative?

545. Where are you now?

546. Why quality management?

547. What personnel are the change agents for your initiative?

548. Have the frequency of collection and the points in the process where measurements will be made been determined?

549. Does your process ensure quality?

550. What lessons have you learned so far?

551. Are you following the quality standards?

552. Are you making progress on the goals?

553. Where do you want to be?

554. What personnel are the sponsors for that initiative?

555. Purpose of goal: the motive is determined by asking, why do you want to achieve this goal?

556. The motive is determined by asking, Why do you want to achieve this goal?

2.27 Responsibility Assignment Matrix: Infrastructure Decisions

557. Are all authorized tasks assigned to identified organizational elements?

558. What is the purpose of assigning and documenting responsibility?

559. Availability – will the group or the person be available within the necessary time interval?

560. Are material costs reported within the same period as that in which BCWP is earned for that material?

561. Evaluate the impact of schedule changes, work around, etc?

562. No rs: if a task has no one listed as responsible, who is getting the job done?

563. What do you do when people do not respond?

564. Will too many Signing-off responsibilities delay the completion of the activity/deliverable?

565. Will too many Communicating responsibilities tangle the Infrastructure Decisions project in unnecessary communications?

566. Are indirect costs charged to the appropriate indirect pools and incurring organization?

567. Performance to date and material commitment?

568. Are people encouraged to bring up issues?

569. Contract line items and end items?

570. Are meaningful indicators identified for use in measuring the status of cost and schedule performance?

571. Most people let you know when others re too busy, and are others really too busy?

572. What expertise is available in your department?

573. Does the scheduling system identify in a timely manner the status of work?

2.28 Roles and Responsibilities: Infrastructure Decisions

574. Implementation of actions: Who are the responsible units?

575. Key conclusions and recommendations: Are conclusions and recommendations relevant and acceptable?

576. What should you do now to prepare for your career 5+ years from now?

577. What is working well?

578. How is your work-life balance?

579. Was the expectation clearly communicated?

580. Attainable / achievable: the goal is attainable; can you actually accomplish the goal?

581. Are Infrastructure Decisions project team roles and responsibilities identified and documented?

582. Is feedback clearly communicated and non-judgmental?

583. Authority: what areas/Infrastructure Decisions projects in your work do you have the authority to decide upon and act on the already stated decisions?

584. Once the responsibilities are defined for the

Infrastructure Decisions project, have the deliverables, roles and responsibilities been clearly communicated to every participant?

585. Do the values and practices inherent in the culture of your organization foster or hinder the process?

586. Be specific; avoid generalities. Thank you and great work alone are insufficient. What exactly do you appreciate and why?

587. Once the responsibilities are defined for the Infrastructure Decisions project, have the deliverables, roles and responsibilities been clearly communicated to every participant?

588. Required skills, knowledge, experience?

589. What expectations were NOT met?

590. What specific behaviors did you observe?

591. What should you highlight for improvement?

2.29 Human Resource Management Plan: Infrastructure Decisions

592. List the assumptions made to date. What did you have to assume to be true to complete the charter?

593. Timeline and milestones?

594. Have the key functions and capabilities been defined and assigned to each release or iteration?

595. Infrastructure Decisions project definition & scope?

596. Are trade-offs between accepting the risk and mitigating the risk identified?

597. Are decisions captured in a decisions log?

598. Pareto diagrams, statistical sampling, flow charting or trend analysis used quality monitoring?

599. Is current scope of the Infrastructure Decisions project substantially different than that originally defined?

600. Where is your organization headed?

601. Has a structured approach been used to break work effort into manageable components (WBS)?

602. Infrastructure Decisions project Objectives?

603. What were things that you need to improve?

604. Have all team members been part of identifying risks?

605. Are Infrastructure Decisions project contact logs kept up to date?

606. Do Infrastructure Decisions project managers participating in the Infrastructure Decisions project know the Infrastructure Decisions projects true status first hand?

607. Are all payments made according to the contract(s)?

608. Does the resource management plan include a personnel development plan?

2.30 Communications Management Plan: Infrastructure Decisions

609. Will messages be directly related to the release strategy or phases of the Infrastructure Decisions project?

610. Who will use or be affected by the result of a Infrastructure Decisions project?

611. What approaches to you feel are the best ones to use?

612. How do you manage communications?

613. Who is responsible?

614. Who are the members of the governing body?

615. What communications method?

616. In your work, how much time is spent on stakeholder identification?

617. Who is involved as you identify stakeholders?

618. What data is going to be required?

619. What is the stakeholders level of authority?

620. Do you then often overlook a key stakeholder or stakeholder group?

621. Are there too many who have an interest in some aspect of your work?

622. Are you constantly rushing from meeting to meeting?

623. What approaches do you use?

624. Conflict resolution -which method when?

625. Who have you worked with in past, similar initiatives?

626. Do you have members of your team responsible for certain stakeholders?

627. Are others needed?

2.31 Risk Management Plan: Infrastructure Decisions

628. What will the damage be?

629. Does the Infrastructure Decisions project have the authority and ability to avoid the risk?

630. What things might go wrong?

631. How quickly does each item need to be resolved?

632. Mitigation -how can you avoid the risk?

633. What is the likelihood that your organization would accept responsibility for the risk?

634. Costs associated with late delivery or a defective product?

635. Internal technical and management reviews?

636. Can the Infrastructure Decisions project proceed without assuming the risk?

637. Is the customer willing to participate in reviews?

638. How is risk identification performed?

639. Are testing tools available and suitable?

640. What are the cost, schedule and resource impacts of avoiding the risk?

641. Are people attending meetings and doing work?

642. My Infrastructure Decisions project leader has suddenly left your organization, what do you do?

643. What is the cost to the Infrastructure Decisions project if it does occur?

644. How is risk response planning performed?

645. Degree of confidence in estimated size estimate?

646. How can the process be made more effective or less cumbersome (process improvements)?

2.32 Risk Register: Infrastructure Decisions

647. When will it happen?

648. What is the reason for current performance gaps and do the risks and opportunities identified previously account for this?

649. Manageability – have mitigations to the risk been identified?

650. What may happen or not go according to plan?

651. How could corresponding Risk affect the Infrastructure Decisions project in terms of cost and schedule?

652. How are risks identified?

653. What evidence do you have to justify the likelihood score of the risk (audit, incident report, claim, complaints, inspection, internal review)?

654. Preventative actions - planned actions to reduce the likelihood a risk will occur and/or reduce the seriousness should it occur. What should you do now?

655. What are your key risks/show istoppers and what is being done to manage them?

656. Technology risk -is the Infrastructure Decisions project technically feasible?

657. Is further information required before making a decision?

658. What further options might be available for responding to the risk?

659. How is a Community Risk Register created?

660. What action, if any, has been taken to respond to the risk?

661. How are risks graded?

662. Market risk -will the new service or product be useful to your organization or marketable to others?

663. Risk probability and impact: how will the probabilities and impacts of risk items be assessed?

664. Are corrective measures implemented as planned?

665. Assume the risk event or situation happens, what would the impact be?

666. What are the main aims, objectives of the policy, strategy, or service and the intended outcomes?

2.33 Probability and Impact Assessment: Infrastructure Decisions

667. How do you maximize short-term return on investment?

668. Are requirements fully understood by the software engineering team and customers?

669. Are the software tools integrated with each other?

670. Are trained personnel, including supervisors and Infrastructure Decisions project managers, available to handle such a large Infrastructure Decisions project?

671. Are flexibility and reuse paramount?

672. What would be the effect of slippage?

673. Anticipated volatility of the requirements?

674. Are Infrastructure Decisions project requirements stable?

675. How would you assess the risk management process in the Infrastructure Decisions project?

676. How is risk handled within this Infrastructure Decisions project organization?

677. Are the facilities, expertise, resources, and

management know-how available to handle the situation?

678. Which risks need to move on to Perform Quantitative Risk Analysis?

679. How much is the probability of a risk occurring?

680. Is there additional information that would make you more confident about your analysis?

681. How solid is the Infrastructure Decisions projection of competitive reaction?

682. What things are likely to change?

683. Are staff committed for the duration of the Infrastructure Decisions project?

684. How will economic events and trends likely affect the Infrastructure Decisions project?

685. What are its business ethics?

686. What is the experience (performance, attitude, business ethics, etc.) in the past with contractors?

2.34 Probability and Impact Matrix: Infrastructure Decisions

687. Is the present organizational structure for handling the Infrastructure Decisions project sufficient?

688. How do you define a risk?

689. What new technologies are being explored in the same area?

690. Do the people have the right combinations of skills?

691. What will be the environmental impact of the Infrastructure Decisions project?

692. What can you use the analyzed risks for?

693. Mandated specific features?

694. The customer requests a change to the Infrastructure Decisions project that would increase the Infrastructure Decisions project risk. Which should you do before ass the others?

695. How solid is the Infrastructure Decisions projection of competitive reaction?

696. How well is the risk understood?

697. Can you handle the investment risk?

698. How is the Infrastructure Decisions project going to be managed?

699. What would be the best solution?

700. Risk categorization -which of your categories has more risk than others?

701. What are the current demands of the customer?

702. How can you understand and diagnose risks and identify sources?

703. Is the Infrastructure Decisions project cutting across the entire organization?

704. What should be the level of coordination?

2.35 Risk Data Sheet: Infrastructure Decisions

705. Do effective diagnostic tests exist?

706. Risk of what?

707. What is the environment within which you operate (social trends, economic, community values, broad based participation, national directions etc.)?

708. Has a sensitivity analysis been carried out?

709. If it happens, what are the consequences?

710. What are the main threats to your existence?

711. What were the Causes that contributed?

712. What will be the consequences if the risk happens?

713. How can it happen?

714. What is the chance that it will happen?

715. What do you know?

716. What are you trying to achieve (Objectives)?

717. Potential for recurrence?

718. Type of risk identified?

719. What can happen?

720. Whom do you serve (customers)?

721. What do people affected think about the need for, and practicality of preventive measures?

722. What will be the consequences if it happens?

2.36 Procurement Management Plan: Infrastructure Decisions

723. Does the Infrastructure Decisions project have a Quality Culture?

724. Are action items captured and managed?

725. Are multiple estimation methods being employed?

726. Are the schedule estimates reasonable given the Infrastructure Decisions project?

727. Was the Infrastructure Decisions project schedule reviewed by all stakeholders and formally accepted?

728. What are things that you need to improve?

729. Is there an onboarding process in place?

730. Are milestone deliverables effectively tracked and compared to Infrastructure Decisions project plan?

731. Are internal Infrastructure Decisions project status meetings held at reasonable intervals?

732. Have all documents been archived in a Infrastructure Decisions project repository for each release?

733. Have all involved Infrastructure Decisions project

stakeholders and work groups committed to the Infrastructure Decisions project?

734. Are Infrastructure Decisions project leaders committed to this Infrastructure Decisions project full time?

735. In which phase of the Acquisition Process Cycle does source qualifications reside?

736. Has the Infrastructure Decisions project manager been identified?

737. Are decisions made in a timely manner?

738. Have external dependencies been captured in the schedule?

739. Are Infrastructure Decisions project team members committed fulltime?

740. What were things that you did very well and want to do the same again on the next Infrastructure Decisions project?

741. Public engagement – did you get it right?

2.37 Source Selection Criteria: Infrastructure Decisions

742. Is this a cost contract?

743. How can business terms and conditions be improved to yield more effective price competition?

744. Does the evaluation of any change include an impact analysis; how will the change affect the scope, time, cost, and quality of the goods or services being provided?

745. What benefits are accrued from issuing a DRFP in advance of issuing a final RFP?

746. Can you reasonably estimate total organization requirements for the coming year?

747. How should the oral presentations be handled?

748. Do proposed hours support content and schedule?

749. Can you identify proposed teaming partners and/or subcontractors and consider the nature and extent of proposed involvement in satisfying the Infrastructure Decisions project requirements?

750. Do you consider all weaknesses, significant weaknesses, and deficiencies?

751. How much past performance information should

be requested?

752. What evidence should be provided regarding proposal evaluations?

753. How do you manage procurement?

754. Is there collaboration among your evaluators?

755. How should oral presentations be prepared for?

756. Comparison of each offers prices to the estimated prices -are there significant differences?

757. Do you have designated specific forms or worksheets?

758. What should be considered?

759. What should be the contracting officers strategy?

760. What instructions should be provided regarding oral presentations?

761. What information may not be provided?

2.38 Stakeholder Management Plan: Infrastructure Decisions

762. How will the equipment be verified?

763. What is to be the method of release?

764. Are there any potential occupational health and safety issues due to the proposed purchases?

765. Does the Infrastructure Decisions project have a Quality Culture?

766. Is a pmo (Infrastructure Decisions project management office) in place and does it provide oversight to the Infrastructure Decisions project?

767. What are the criteria for selecting suppliers of off the shelf products?

768. Is there an on-going process in place to monitor Infrastructure Decisions project risks?

769. Has the business need been clearly defined?

770. Has the Infrastructure Decisions project manager been identified?

771. What guidelines or procedures currently exist that must be adhered to (eg departmental accounting procedures)?

772. What is the primary function of the Activity

Decomposition Decision Tree?

773. Has a quality assurance plan been developed for the Infrastructure Decisions project?

774. What sources of information are reliable?

775. Where are the verification requirements to be documented (eg purchase order, agreement etc)?

776. Are all vendor contracts closed out?

777. Are mitigation strategies identified?

778. What other teams / processes would be impacted by changes to the current process, and how?

779. Are schedule deliverables actually delivered?

2.39 Change Management Plan: Infrastructure Decisions

780. How much change management is needed?

781. What prerequisite knowledge or training is required?

782. Has this been negotiated with the customer and sponsor?

783. What prerequisite knowledge do corresponding groups need?

784. Is it the same for each of the business units?

785. Are there any restrictions on who can receive the communications?

786. What method and medium would you use to announce a message?

787. Will all field readiness criteria have been practically met prior to training roll-out?

788. Who is responsible for which tasks?

789. Change invariability confront many relationships especially the already stated that require a set of behaviours What roles with in your organization are affected and how?

790. What goal(s) do you hope to accomplish?

791. Have the systems been configured and tested?

792. What can you do to minimise misinterpretation and negative perceptions?

793. Will the culture embrace or reject this change?

794. What risks may occur upfront?

795. What roles within your organization are affected, and how?

796. What relationships will change?

797. How far reaching in your organization is the change?

798. What are you trying to achieve as a result of communication?

799. What do you expect the target audience to do, say, think or feel as a result of this communication?

3.0 Executing Process Group: Infrastructure Decisions

800. What are deliverables of your Infrastructure Decisions project?

801. What is involved in the solicitation process?

802. How does a Infrastructure Decisions project life cycle differ from a product life cycle?

803. Will outside resources be needed to help?

804. How can software assist in procuring goods and services?

805. Is the Infrastructure Decisions project performing better or worse than planned?

806. After how many days will the lease cost be the same as the purchase cost for the equipment?

807. On which process should team members spend the most time?

808. Is activity definition the first process involved in Infrastructure Decisions project time management?

809. What are the main parts of the scope statement?

810. How do you enter durations, link tasks, and view critical path information?

811. Would you rate yourself as being risk-averse, risk-neutral, or risk-seeking?

812. Based on your Infrastructure Decisions project communication management plan, what worked well?

813. Why is it important to determine activity sequencing on Infrastructure Decisions projects?

814. Do your results resemble a normal distribution?

815. Do the partners have sufficient financial capacity to keep up the benefits produced by the programme?

816. What areas does the group agree are the biggest success on the Infrastructure Decisions project?

3.1 Team Member Status Report: Infrastructure Decisions

817. Does every department have to have a Infrastructure Decisions project Manager on staff?

818. The problem with Reward & Recognition Programs is that the truly deserving people all too often get left out. How can you make it practical?

819. How will resource planning be done?

820. How does this product, good, or service meet the needs of the Infrastructure Decisions project and your organization as a whole?

821. Are your organizations Infrastructure Decisions projects more successful over time?

822. Does the product, good, or service already exist within your organization?

823. How it is to be done?

824. Why is it to be done?

825. What is to be done?

826. How much risk is involved?

827. Do you have an Enterprise Infrastructure Decisions project Management Office (EPMO)?

828. How can you make it practical?

829. Are the attitudes of staff regarding Infrastructure Decisions project work improving?

830. When a teams productivity and success depend on collaboration and the efficient flow of information, what generally fails them?

831. Is there evidence that staff is taking a more professional approach toward management of your organizations Infrastructure Decisions projects?

832. Will the staff do training or is that done by a third party?

833. Are the products of your organizations Infrastructure Decisions projects meeting customers objectives?

834. Does your organization have the means (staff, money, contract, etc.) to produce or to acquire the product, good, or service?

835. What specific interest groups do you have in place?

3.2 Change Request: Infrastructure Decisions

836. What are the Impacts to your organization?

837. How do team members communicate with each other?

838. What is the relationship between requirements attributes and attributes like complexity and size?

839. Who is included in the change control team?

840. Are you implementing itil processes?

841. How to get changes (code) out in a timely manner?

842. How are changes requested (forms, method of communication)?

843. Should staff call into the helpdesk or go to the website?

844. Has the change been highlighted and documented in the CSCI?

845. What mechanism is used to appraise others of changes that are made?

846. Who is responsible to authorize changes?

847. Are there requirements attributes that are

strongly related to the complexity and size?

848. How do you get changes (code) out in a timely manner?

849. When to submit a change request?

850. What is the purpose of change control?

851. What are the requirements for urgent changes?

852. How many times must the change be modified or presented to the change control board before it is approved?

853. Who can suggest changes?

854. For which areas does this operating procedure apply?

855. Is it feasible to use requirements attributes as predictors of reliability?

3.3 Change Log: Infrastructure Decisions

856. Is the change request within Infrastructure Decisions project scope?

857. Is the change request open, closed or pending?

858. When was the request approved?

859. When was the request submitted?

860. Will the Infrastructure Decisions project fail if the change request is not executed?

861. Is the change backward compatible without limitations?

862. Is this a mandatory replacement?

863. How does this relate to the standards developed for specific business processes?

864. Do the described changes impact on the integrity or security of the system?

865. Where do changes come from?

866. Does the suggested change request seem to represent a necessary enhancement to the product?

867. Who initiated the change request?

868. How does this change affect scope?

869. Does the suggested change request represent a desired enhancement to the products functionality?

870. How does this change affect the timeline of the schedule?

871. Is the requested change request a result of changes in other Infrastructure Decisions project(s)?

872. Is the submitted change a new change or a modification of a previously approved change?

3.4 Decision Log: Infrastructure Decisions

873. Meeting purpose; why does this team meet?

874. Decision-making process; how will the team make decisions?

875. Linked to original objective?

876. What was the rationale for the decision?

877. It becomes critical to track and periodically revisit both operational effectiveness; Are you noticing all that you need to, and are you interpreting what you see effectively?

878. How do you know when you are achieving it?

879. Who is the decisionmaker?

880. What eDiscovery problem or issue did your organization set out to fix or make better?

881. What alternatives/risks were considered?

882. How effective is maintaining the log at facilitating organizational learning?

883. What are the cost implications?

884. How does an increasing emphasis on cost containment influence the strategies and tactics

used?

885. Adversarial environment. is your opponent open to a non-traditional workflow, or will it likely challenge anything you do?

886. How does the use a Decision Support System influence the strategies/tactics or costs?

887. Is your opponent open to a non-traditional workflow, or will it likely challenge anything you do?

888. Which variables make a critical difference?

889. At what point in time does loss become unacceptable?

890. How do you define success?

891. How consolidated and comprehensive a story can you tell by capturing currently available incident data in a central location and through a log of key decisions during an incident?

892. Who will be given a copy of this document and where will it be kept?

3.5 Quality Audit: Infrastructure Decisions

893. Do the suppliers use a formal quality system?

894. How does your organization know that its staff support services planning and management systems are appropriately effective and constructive?

895. How does your organization know that its research programs are appropriately effective and constructive?

896. How does your organization know that its management of its ethical responsibilities is appropriately effective and constructive?

897. Do all staff have the necessary authority and resources to deliver what is expected of them?

898. Is your organizations resource allocation system properly aligned with its collection of intentions?

899. How does your organization know that its system for recruiting the best staff possible are appropriately effective and constructive?

900. How does your organization know that its processes for managing severance are appropriately effective, constructive and fair?

901. What happens if your organization fails its Quality Audit?

902. Are measuring and test equipment that have been placed out of service suitably identified and excluded from use in any device reconditioning operation?

903. Why are you trying to do it?

904. Are all staff empowered and encouraged to contribute to ongoing improvement efforts?

905. How are you auditing your organizations compliance with regulations?

906. Are all areas associated with the storage and reconditioning of devices clean, free of rubbish, adequately ventilated and in good repair?

907. How does the organization know that its system for maintaining and advancing the capabilities of its staff, particularly in relation to the Mission of the organization, is appropriately effective and constructive?

908. How does your organization know that its staff embody the core knowledge, skills and characteristics for which it wishes to be recognized?

909. Does the report read coherently?

910. What is the collective experience of the team to be assigned to an audit?

911. Are storage areas and reconditioning operations designed to prevent mix-ups and assure orderly handling of both the distressed and reconditioned

devices?

912. How does your organization know that its systems for assisting staff with career planning and employment placements are appropriately effective and constructive?

3.6 Team Directory: Infrastructure Decisions

913. Process decisions: which organizational elements and which individuals will be assigned management functions?

914. Process decisions: are all start-up, turn over and close out requirements of the contract satisfied?

915. Who will be the stakeholders on your next Infrastructure Decisions project?

916. Have you decided when to celebrate the Infrastructure Decisions projects completion date?

917. How and in what format should information be presented?

918. Decisions: is the most suitable form of contract being used?

919. Who will write the meeting minutes and distribute?

920. Where will the product be used and/or delivered or built when appropriate?

921. Who are the Team Members?

922. How will the team handle changes?

923. What are you going to deliver or accomplish?

924. How do unidentified risks impact the outcome of the Infrastructure Decisions project?

925. Do purchase specifications and configurations match requirements?

926. Does a Infrastructure Decisions project team directory list all resources assigned to the Infrastructure Decisions project?

927. Timing: when do the effects of communication take place?

928. Is construction on schedule?

929. When does information need to be distributed?

930. Process decisions: how well was task order work performed?

931. Who will talk to the customer?

3.7 Team Operating Agreement: Infrastructure Decisions

932. What is the number of cases currently teamed?

933. Do you listen for voice tone and word choice to understand the meaning behind words?

934. What individual strengths does each team member bring to the group?

935. Resource allocation: how will individual team members account for time and expenses, and how will this be allocated in the team budget?

936. Do you call or email participants to ensure understanding, follow-through and commitment to the meeting outcomes?

937. What resources can be provided for the team in terms of equipment, space, time for training, protected time and space for meetings, and travel allowances?

938. Seconds for members to respond?

939. How does teaming fit in with overall organizational goals and meet organizational needs?

940. What are some potential sources of conflict among team members?

941. Do team members reside in more than two

countries?

942. Did you delegate tasks such as taking meeting minutes, presenting a topic and soliciting input?

943. Did you prepare participants for the next meeting?

944. To whom do you deliver your services?

945. What is your unique contribution to your organization?

946. How will you divide work equitably?

947. Do you brief absent members after they view meeting notes or listen to a recording?

948. Are there differences in access to communication and collaboration technology based on team member location?

949. What is culture?

950. Do you ensure that all participants know how to use the required technology?

951. Do you record meetings for the already stated unable to attend?

3.8 Team Performance Assessment: Infrastructure Decisions

952. How do you manage human resources?

953. To what degree can team members vigorously define the teams purpose in considerations with others who are not part of the functioning team?

954. Do friends perform better than acquaintances?

955. How hard do you try to make a good selection?

956. How hard did you try to make a good selection?

957. How much interpersonal friction is there in your team?

958. To what degree do team members understand one anothers roles and skills?

959. To what degree can team members frequently and easily communicate with one another?

960. To what degree will the team adopt a concrete, clearly understood, and agreed-upon approach that will result in achievement of the teams goals?

961. To what degree are staff involved as partners in the improvement process?

962. To what degree are the members clear on what they are individually responsible for and what they

are jointly responsible for?

963. To what degree does the teams work approach provide opportunity for members to engage in open interaction?

964. To what degree will the team ensure that all members equitably share the work essential to the success of the team?

965. Individual task proficiency and team process behavior: what is important for team functioning?

966. To what degree is there a sense that only the team can succeed?

967. Delaying market entry: how long is too long?

968. To what degree does the teams purpose constitute a broader, deeper aspiration than just accomplishing short-term goals?

969. Social categorization and intergroup behaviour: Does minimal intergroup discrimination make social identity more positive?

970. What is method variance?

971. To what degree does the teams work approach provide opportunity for members to engage in fact-based problem solving?

3.9 Team Member Performance Assessment: Infrastructure Decisions

972. What are the standards or expectations for success?

973. What are best practices in use for the performance measurement system?

974. How is performance assessment used in making future award decisions including options and extend/compete decisions?

975. What is a general description of the processes under performance measurement and assessment?

976. Does the rater (supervisor) have the authority or responsibility to tell an employee that the employees performance is unsatisfactory?

977. What is needed for effective data teams?

978. What kinds of performance factors / elements do you use?

979. Are the goals SMART ?

980. What qualities does a successful Team leader possess?

981. Does statute or regulation require the job responsibility?

982. To what extent are systems and applications (e.g., game engine, mobile device platform) utilized?

983. Why do performance reviews?

984. Does adaptive training work?

985. How often should assessments be conducted?

986. How are assessments designed, delivered, and otherwise used to maximize training?

987. To what degree can all members engage in open and interactive considerations?

988. Are any validation activities performed?

989. To what degree do team members frequently explore the teams purpose and its implications?

990. How do you implement Cost Reduction?

3.10 Issue Log: Infrastructure Decisions

991. How much time does it take to do it?

992. Who is the issue assigned to?

993. Do you prepare stakeholder engagement plans?

994. Is access to the Issue Log controlled?

995. What steps can you take for positive relationships?

996. Are stakeholder roles recognized by your organization?

997. What effort will a change need?

998. Is the issue log kept in a safe place?

999. Do you often overlook a key stakeholder or stakeholder group?

1000. What is the impact on the risks?

1001. What is the status of the issue?

1002. How often do you engage with stakeholders?

1003. Who were proponents/opponents?

1004. What are the typical contents?

1005. Who reported the issue?

1006. Are the stakeholders getting the information they need, are they consulted, are concerns addressed?

1007. Which team member will work with each stakeholder?

4.0 Monitoring and Controlling Process Group: Infrastructure Decisions

1008. Did you implement the program as designed?

1009. How well did the team follow the chosen processes?

1010. Is the verbiage used appropriate and understandable?

1011. Did the Infrastructure Decisions project team have enough people to execute the Infrastructure Decisions project plan?

1012. Based on your Infrastructure Decisions project communication management plan, what worked well?

1013. What good practices or successful experiences or transferable examples have been identified?

1014. Measurable - are the targets measurable?

1015. How can you monitor progress?

1016. What is the timeline?

1017. Who needs to be involved in the planning?

1018. Are there areas that need improvement?

1019. Did the Infrastructure Decisions project team have the right skills?

1020. How well did the chosen processes produce the expected results?

1021. What resources are necessary?

1022. Were escalated issues resolved promptly?

1023. Key stakeholders to work with. How many potential communications channels exist on the Infrastructure Decisions project?

1024. Have operating capacities been created and/or reinforced in partners?

1025. Is the schedule for the set products being met?

4.1 Project Performance Report: Infrastructure Decisions

1026. To what degree does the team possess adequate membership to achieve its ends?

1027. To what degree does the informal organization make use of individual resources and meet individual needs?

1028. To what degree does the task meet individual needs?

1029. To what degree are the goals realistic?

1030. How can Infrastructure Decisions project sustainability be maintained?

1031. What is the PRS?

1032. To what degree will the approach capitalize on and enhance the skills of all team members in a manner that takes into consideration other demands on members of the team?

1033. To what degree is there centralized control of information sharing?

1034. To what degree are the skill areas critical to team performance present?

1035. To what degree will team members, individually and collectively, commit time to help themselves and others learn and develop skills?

1036. To what degree is the information network consistent with the structure of the formal organization?

1037. To what degree are the structures of the formal organization consistent with the behaviors in the informal organization?

1038. What is the degree to which rules govern information exchange between individuals within your organization?

1039. What is in it for you?

1040. To what degree is the team cognizant of small wins to be celebrated along the way?

1041. To what degree do the goals specify concrete team work products?

1042. To what degree are sub-teams possible or necessary?

4.2 Variance Analysis: Infrastructure Decisions

1043. Do work packages consist of discrete tasks which are adequately described?

1044. What should management do?

1045. Is all contract work included in the CWBS?

1046. There are detailed schedules which support control account and work package start and completion dates/events?

1047. How do you identify and isolate causes of favorable and unfavorable cost and schedule variances?

1048. Are there quarterly budgets with quarterly performance comparisons?

1049. Are all elements of indirect expense identified to overhead cost budgets of Infrastructure Decisions projections?

1050. Are there changes in the direct base to which overhead costs are allocated?

1051. Are overhead cost budgets established for each department which has authority to incur overhead costs?

1052. Are procedures for variance analysis

documented and consistently applied at the control account level and selected WBS and organizational levels at least monthly as a routine task?

1053. What is the total budget for the Infrastructure Decisions project (including estimates for authorized and unpriced work)?

1054. Are work packages assigned to performing organizations?

1055. Is work properly classified as measured effort, LOE, or apportioned effort and appropriately separated?

1056. How are material, labor, and overhead standards set?

1057. Are overhead costs budgets established on a basis consistent with the anticipated direct business base?

1058. Wbs elements contractually specified for reporting of status to your organization (lowest level only)?

1059. Are the overhead pools formally and adequately identified?

1060. Are all cwbs elements specified for external reporting?

1061. Does the contractors system identify work accomplishment against the schedule plan?

1062. How do you manage changes in the nature of

the overhead requirements?

4.3 Earned Value Status: Infrastructure Decisions

1063. Validation is a process of ensuring that the developed system will actually achieve the stakeholders desired outcomes; Are you building the right product? What do you validate?

1064. Where is evidence-based earned value in your organization reported?

1065. What is the unit of forecast value?

1066. If earned value management (EVM) is so good in determining the true status of a Infrastructure Decisions project and Infrastructure Decisions project its completion, why is it that hardly any one uses it in information systems related Infrastructure Decisions projects?

1067. Where are your problem areas?

1068. How much is it going to cost by the finish?

1069. Are you hitting your Infrastructure Decisions projects targets?

1070. Verification is a process of ensuring that the developed system satisfies the stakeholders agreements and specifications; Are you building the product right? What do you verify?

1071. How does this compare with other

Infrastructure Decisions projects?

1072. Earned value can be used in almost any Infrastructure Decisions project situation and in almost any Infrastructure Decisions project environment. it may be used on large Infrastructure Decisions projects, medium sized Infrastructure Decisions projects, tiny Infrastructure Decisions projects (in cut-down form), complex and simple Infrastructure Decisions projects and in any market sector. some people, of course, know all about earned value, they have used it for years - but perhaps not as effectively as they could have?

1073. When is it going to finish?

4.4 Risk Audit: Infrastructure Decisions

1074. How effective are your risk controls?

1075. When your organization is entering into a major contract, does it seek legal advice?

1076. How do you govern assets?

1077. Can assurance be expanded beyond the traditional audit without undermining independence?

1078. Auditor independence: a burdensome constraint or a core value?

1079. Level of preparation and skill?

1080. Estimated size of product in number of programs, files, transactions?

1081. How are risk appetites expressed?

1082. Number of users of the product?

1083. What limitations do auditors face in effectively applying risk-assessment results to the risk of material misstatement measures?

1084. Is your organization able to present documentary evidence in support of compliance?

1085. Has everyone (staff, volunteers and participants)

agreed to a code of behaviour or conduct?

1086. What are the commonly used work arounds in high risk areas?

1087. Are you meeting your legal, regulatory and compliance requirements - if not, why not?

1088. Does the Infrastructure Decisions project team have experience with the technology to be implemented?

1089. If applicable; which route/packaging option do you choose for transport of hazmat material?

1090. Do you promote education and training opportunities?

1091. Do you have an emergency plan?

1092. Do you have an understanding of insurance claims processes?

4.5 Contractor Status Report: Infrastructure Decisions

1093. What process manages the contracts?

1094. What was the final actual cost?

1095. What was the actual budget or estimated cost for your organizations services?

1096. Describe how often regular updates are made to the proposed solution. Are corresponding regular updates included in the standard maintenance plan?

1097. How does the proposed individual meet each requirement?

1098. What was the overall budget or estimated cost?

1099. What was the budget or estimated cost for your organizations services?

1100. What is the average response time for answering a support call?

1101. If applicable; describe your standard schedule for new software version releases. Are new software version releases included in the standard maintenance plan?

1102. How long have you been using the services?

1103. How is risk transferred?

1104. What are the minimum and optimal bandwidth requirements for the proposed solution?

1105. Who can list a Infrastructure Decisions project as organization experience, your organization or a previous employee of your organization?

1106. Are there contractual transfer concerns?

4.6 Formal Acceptance: Infrastructure Decisions

1107. Was business value realized?

1108. Did the Infrastructure Decisions project manager and team act in a professional and ethical manner?

1109. Who supplies data?

1110. Do you perform formal acceptance or burn-in tests?

1111. General estimate of the costs and times to complete the Infrastructure Decisions project?

1112. Did the Infrastructure Decisions project achieve its MOV?

1113. Was the sponsor/customer satisfied?

1114. Is formal acceptance of the Infrastructure Decisions project product documented and distributed?

1115. What can you do better next time?

1116. Does it do what Infrastructure Decisions project team said it would?

1117. What was done right?

1118. Who would use it?

1119. Does it do what client said it would?

1120. Do you buy pre-configured systems or build your own configuration?

1121. What is the Acceptance Management Process?

1122. Was the Infrastructure Decisions project goal achieved?

1123. Do you buy-in installation services?

1124. What are the requirements against which to test, Who will execute?

1125. What features, practices, and processes proved to be strengths or weaknesses?

1126. What function(s) does it fill or meet?

5.0 Closing Process Group: Infrastructure Decisions

1127. What will you do?

1128. How well defined and documented were the Infrastructure Decisions project management processes you chose to use?

1129. What is the risk of failure to your organization?

1130. Is this an updated Infrastructure Decisions project Proposal Document?

1131. What could have been improved?

1132. What went well?

1133. Based on your Infrastructure Decisions project communication management plan, what worked well?

1134. Is the Infrastructure Decisions project funded?

1135. How critical is the Infrastructure Decisions project success to the success of your organization?

1136. Are there funding or time constraints?

1137. Can the lesson learned be replicated?

1138. Is this a follow-on to a previous Infrastructure Decisions project?

1139. Did the Infrastructure Decisions project management methodology work?

1140. Did you do what you said you were going to do?

5.1 Procurement Audit: Infrastructure Decisions

1141. Are open purchase orders with a fixed monetary limitation used for local purchases of small dollar value?

1142. Are employees with cash disbursement responsibilities required to take scheduled vacations?

1143. Are the established budget and timetable (milestones) respected?

1144. Is there no evidence of unauthorized release of information or seemingly unnecessary contacts with bidders personnel during the evaluation and negotiation processes?

1145. Did additional works amount to no more than 50% of the initial contract?

1146. Are purchase requisitions used to generate purchase orders?

1147. How do you assess whether the technical and financial evaluation was done properly and in fair manner?

1148. Which contracts have been awarded for works, supply of products or provision of services?

1149. Where your organization engaged an expert, was the contract awarded in compliance with procurement regulations?

1150. Does procurement staff have recognized professional procurement qualifications or sufficient training?

1151. Is the chosen supplier part of your organizations database?

1152. How are you making the audit trail easy to follow?

1153. Was confidentiality ensured when necessary?

1154. Are the internal control systems operational?

1155. Is the procurement function/unit organized the most appropriate way taking into consideration the actual tasks which the department has to carry out?

1156. Are there internal control systems in place to secure that laws and regulations are observed?

1157. Are there policies regarding special approval for capital expenditures?

1158. Is confidentiality guaranteed during the whole process?

1159. Is the procurement Infrastructure Decisions project efficiently managed?

1160. Is there a policy covering the relationship of other departments with vendors?

5.2 Contract Close-Out: Infrastructure Decisions

1161. Have all contract records been included in the Infrastructure Decisions project archives?

1162. Was the contract complete without requiring numerous changes and revisions?

1163. Why Outsource?

1164. Parties: who is involved?

1165. Parties: Authorized?

1166. Are the signers the authorized officials?

1167. How/when used ?

1168. How is the contracting office notified of the automatic contract close-out?

1169. Have all contracts been closed?

1170. Change in circumstances?

1171. What is capture management?

1172. Change in attitude or behavior?

1173. Was the contract sufficiently clear so as not to result in numerous disputes and misunderstandings?

1174. Change in knowledge?

1175. Have all contracts been completed?

1176. How does it work?

1177. What happens to the recipient of services?

1178. Has each contract been audited to verify acceptance and delivery?

1179. Was the contract type appropriate?

1180. Have all acceptance criteria been met prior to final payment to contractors?

5.3 Project or Phase Close-Out: Infrastructure Decisions

1181. What hierarchical authority does the stakeholder have in your organization?

1182. What is the information level of detail required for each stakeholder?

1183. Does the lesson educate others to improve performance?

1184. Who controlled key decisions that were made?

1185. Did the delivered product meet the specified requirements and goals of the Infrastructure Decisions project?

1186. What process was planned for managing issues/risks?

1187. What were the goals and objectives of the communications strategy for the Infrastructure Decisions project?

1188. Were the outcomes different from the already stated planned?

1189. Planned remaining costs?

1190. What were the actual outcomes?

1191. In preparing the Lessons Learned report, should

it reflect a consensus viewpoint, or should the report reflect the different individual viewpoints?

1192. In addition to assessing whether the Infrastructure Decisions project was successful, it is equally critical to analyze why it was or was not fully successful. Are you including this?

1193. Who controlled the resources for the Infrastructure Decisions project?

1194. Were messages directly related to the release strategy or phases of the Infrastructure Decisions project?

1195. Complete yes or no?

1196. What is a Risk?

1197. What information did each stakeholder need to contribute to the Infrastructure Decisions projects success?

1198. Was the user/client satisfied with the end product?

5.4 Lessons Learned: Infrastructure Decisions

1199. What is the impact of tax policy on the case?

1200. Was any formal risk assessment carried out at the start of the Infrastructure Decisions project, and was this followed up during the Infrastructure Decisions project?

1201. What were the success factors?

1202. Does the lesson describe a function that would be done differently the next time?

1203. Were the Infrastructure Decisions project objectives met (if not, briefly account for what wasnt met)?

1204. How was the quality of products/processes assured?

1205. What would you change?

1206. Are there any data that you have overlooked in identifying lessons?

1207. How effectively were issues managed on the Infrastructure Decisions project?

1208. How well did the Infrastructure Decisions project Manager respond to questions or comments related to the Infrastructure Decisions project?

1209. What were the major enablers to a quick response?

1210. Did the Infrastructure Decisions project change significantly?

1211. What was the single greatest success and the single greatest shortcoming or challenge from the Infrastructure Decisions projects perspective?

1212. How timely was the training you received in preparation for the use of the product/service?

1213. What regulatory constraints impact the case?

1214. How much communication is socially oriented?

1215. Is the lesson based on actual Infrastructure Decisions project experience rather than on independent research?

1216. How effective was the quality assurance process?

1217. What is the proportion of in-house and contractor personnel authorized for the Infrastructure Decisions project?

Index

assigned 139, 148, 157, 176, 190, 194, 227, 229-230, 237, 244
assigning 190
Assignment 4, 154, 161, 190
assist 9, 64, 85, 98, 181, 216
assistant 7
assisting 228
associated 144, 198, 227
Assume 194, 201
assuming 198
Assumption 3, 150
assurance 18, 140, 156, 213, 248, 263
assure 227
assured 262
attainable 42, 192
attempted 42
attend 22, 232
attendance 36
attendant 81
attended 36
attending 199
attention 13, 114
attitude 203, 258
attitudes 219
attribute 141, 184
attributes 3, 116, 156, 160, 220-221
audience 215
audiences 185
audited 259
auditing 27, 93, 118, 227
Auditor248
auditors 248
auspices 8
author 1
authority 142, 192, 196, 198, 226, 235, 243, 260
authorize 220
authorized 154, 190, 244, 258, 263
automated 141
automatic 258
available 19, 25, 38, 44, 53, 71, 77, 98, 126, 129, 138, 157, 159-160, 171, 175, 177, 190-191, 198, 201-203, 225
Average 13, 28, 44, 59, 75, 90, 103, 127, 173, 250
avoiding 198

different   7, 20, 30, 32-33, 37, 63-64, 106, 113, 136, 185, 194, 260-261
difficult 67, 159, 161-162, 168, 177
dimensions   24
direct 243-244
direction   31, 48, 139
directions   206
directly 1, 72-73, 196, 261
Directory   5, 229-230
Disagree   12, 17, 29, 45, 60, 76, 92, 105
disaster   47, 56
disclosure   101
discrete   243
discussion   120
displayed   34, 65, 158, 173
disputes   258
disqualify   64
distressed   227
distribute   229
divergent   136
divide 232
Divided   28, 38, 44, 59, 75, 90, 103, 127
division 138
document   11, 131, 143, 150, 184, 225, 254
documented 33, 77, 90, 93, 95, 101, 130, 145, 148, 151, 171, 184, 192, 213, 220, 244, 252, 254
documents   7, 141, 155, 170-171, 186, 208
dollar 256
domains   78
dormant   107
Driver 62
drivers 53
drives 54
driving 116, 124
duration   4, 152, 155, 164, 170-172, 203
durations   30, 216
during 31, 85, 129, 150, 160, 167, 170, 178, 184, 225, 256-257, 262
dynamics   31
earlier 155
earned   6, 190, 246-247
easily 233
economic   203, 206

images 144-145
imbedded   102
impact 5, 38, 45-49, 54, 56, 81, 129, 143-144, 178, 182, 190, 201-
202, 204, 210, 222, 230, 237, 262-263
impacted   129, 213
impacts   47, 58, 151, 172, 198, 201, 220
implement   50, 63, 92, 236, 239
implicit 112
important   21, 23, 29, 72-74, 109, 120, 122, 126, 136, 171,
217, 234
improve   2, 11-12, 61, 76, 78-79, 82-85, 87-90, 129, 131, 168,
185, 195, 208, 260
improved   84, 87, 89, 102, 210, 254
improving   88, 219
incentives   98
incident   200, 225
include   20, 88, 175, 195, 210
included   2, 9, 25, 46, 145, 148, 172-173, 178, 181, 220, 243,
250, 258
INCLUDES   10
including   22, 37, 39, 41, 50, 56, 61, 92-93, 101, 151, 156,
202, 235, 244, 261
increase   82, 109, 204
increased   122
increasing   107, 224
incurred   46
incurring   190
in-depth   9, 12
indicate   64, 97, 109
indicated   94
indicators   19, 57-58, 62, 68, 72-73, 84, 92, 155, 185, 191
indirect   178, 190, 243
indirectly   1
individual   1, 52, 158, 231, 234, 241, 250, 261
industry   97, 109, 121
infinite 111
influence   83, 111, 133, 136, 224-225
informal   241-242
informed   126, 134
ingrained   103
inherent   193
in-house   263
initial   37, 108, 256

process 1-7, 11, 30-32, 39, 41, 43-44, 53, 61-64, 66-74, 80, 83, 93, 96-100, 102-103, 129-130, 134, 136-137, 142, 144-146, 148-151, 155-156, 167, 170, 173, 175, 184-185, 188, 193, 199, 202, 208-209, 212-213, 216, 224, 229-230, 233-234, 239, 246, 250, 253-254, 257, 260, 263
processes 52, 56, 60-64, 66, 68-69, 72, 74-75, 93, 97, 100, 130, 141, 148, 151, 156, 185, 213, 220, 222, 226, 235, 239-240, 249, 253-254, 256, 262
procuring 216
produce 166, 178, 219, 240
produced 68, 78, 217
produces 161
producing 146
product 1, 11, 58, 72-73, 105, 107, 151, 174, 182, 186, 198, 201, 216, 218-219, 222, 229, 246, 248, 252, 260-261, 263
production 35, 122
products 1, 19-20, 46, 125, 132, 135-137, 146, 212, 219, 223, 240, 242, 256, 262
program 22, 73, 100, 134, 136-137, 239
programme 217
programs 218, 226, 248
progress 30, 49, 80, 101, 116, 122, 136-137, 181, 188-189, 239
project 2-4, 6-7, 9, 19, 21-22, 37, 53, 64, 73, 75, 86, 101, 103, 106-109, 112, 114, 119, 121, 124, 128-144, 146, 148-150, 152, 155-162, 164-165, 168, 170-184, 190, 192-196, 198-200, 202-205, 208-210, 212-213, 216-219, 222-223, 229-230, 239-241, 244, 246-247, 249, 251-255, 257-258, 260-263
projection 203-204
projects 2, 48, 115, 128, 130, 135-136, 146, 171, 174, 182, 192, 195, 217-219, 229, 246-247, 261, 263
promising 107
promote 46, 69, 249
promptly 240
proofing 80
proper 101
properly 11, 39, 43, 130, 226, 244, 256
proponents 237
proportion 263
Proposal 211, 254
proposals 95
proposed 45, 82, 89, 139, 143-144, 210, 212, 250-251
protect 64, 123, 138

resolve 18, 23, 25
resolved   140, 198, 240
resource   4, 115, 143, 154, 157, 166-169, 171, 194-195, 198,
218, 226, 231
resources   2, 9, 22, 25, 27, 38, 42, 44, 48, 72, 83, 97-99, 111,
114-115, 124, 129, 135, 139-140, 157, 159-161, 164, 169, 172, 177,
181-182, 202, 216, 226, 230-231, 233, 240-241, 261
respect   1
respected   256
respond   190, 201, 231, 262
responded   13
responding   201
response   22, 28, 94-95, 97, 102, 199, 250, 263
responses   77
responsive   172, 181
result   65, 77-78, 178, 180, 196, 215, 223, 233, 258
resulted   92
resulting   72, 139
results 9, 30, 39, 72, 76, 79, 81-83, 85, 87-89, 92, 97, 136-137, 181,
217, 240, 248
retain   105, 184
retained   67
retention   47
return   78, 108, 202
revenue   22, 48
revenues   48
review 11-12, 35, 67, 175, 183, 186, 200
reviewed   32, 148, 150, 208
reviews 11, 140-141, 148, 165, 176, 198, 236
revised 74, 92
revisions   258
revisit 224
reward 46, 52, 64, 218
rewarded   24
rewards   98
rework 48
rights   1
roll-out 214
routine 98, 244
rubbish 227
rushing 197
safeguard   135
safety   125, 212

297

CPSIA information can be obtained
at www.ICGtesting.com
Printed in the USA
BVHW081943240719
554260BV00012B/609/P